My Book
EX LIBRIS
AF544881
14-

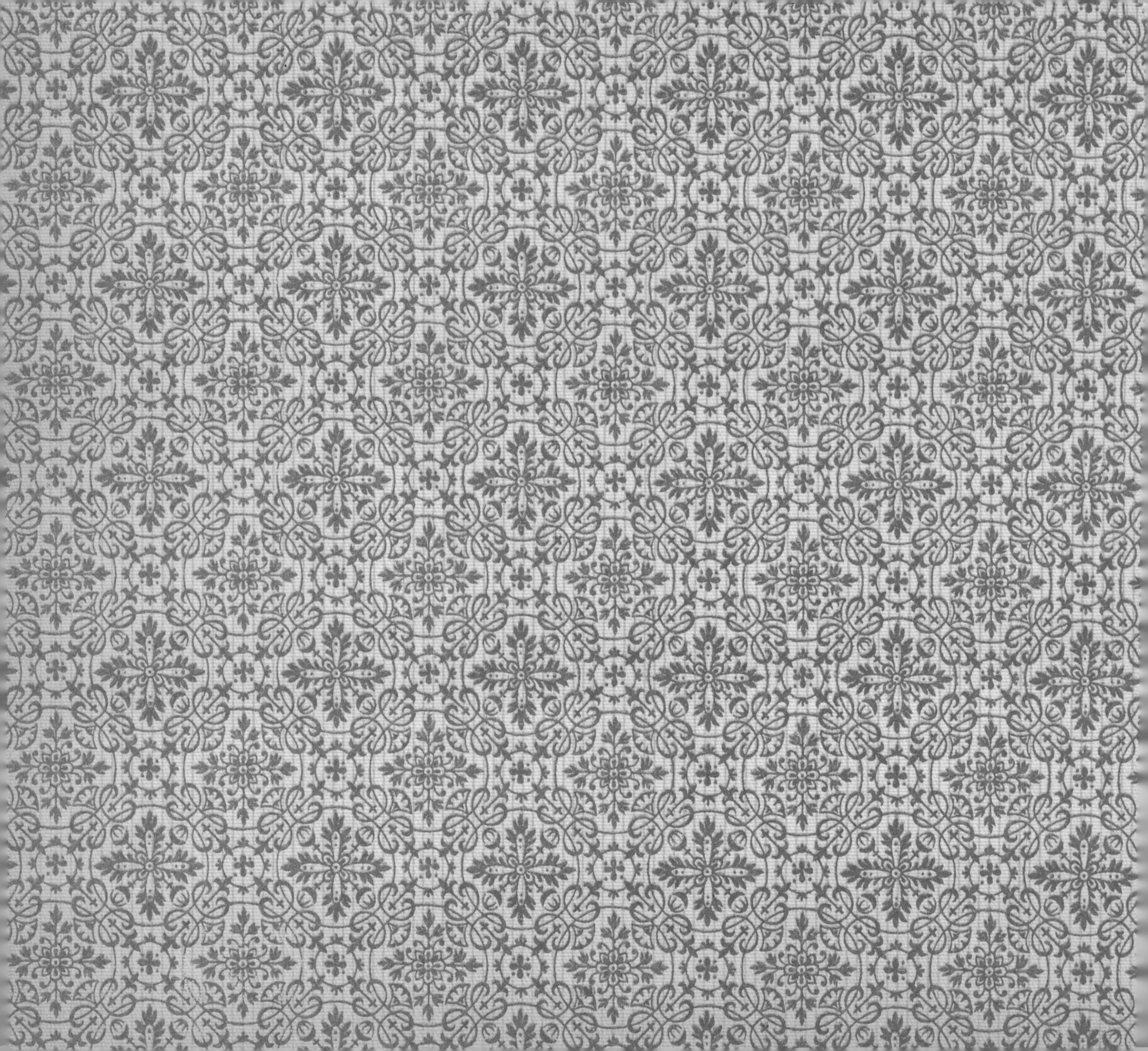

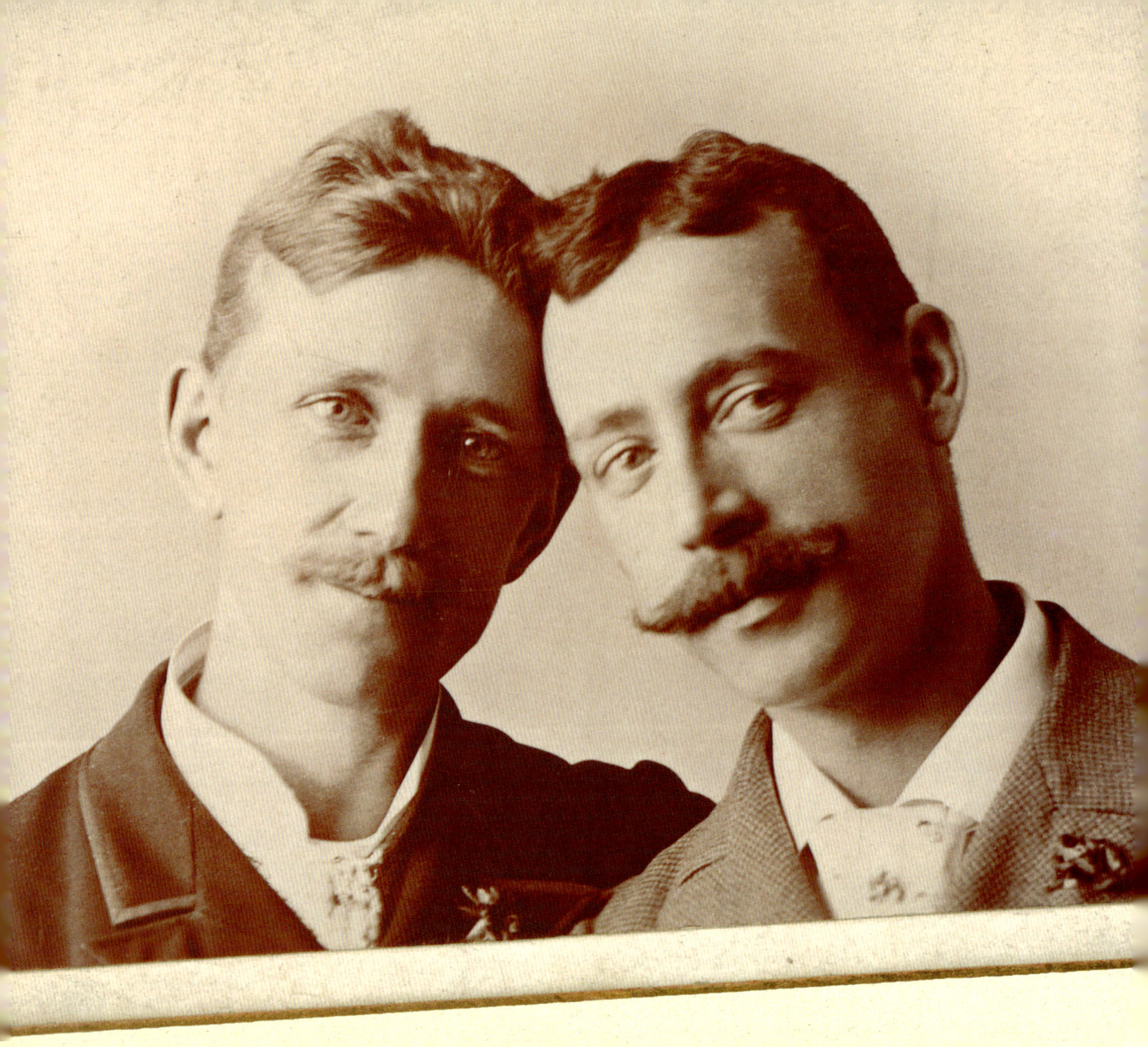

Affectionate Men

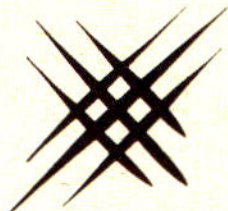

A
PHOTOGRAPHIC
HISTORY
of a
CENTURY
of
MALE
COUPLES
(1850's *to* 1950's)

RUSSELL BUSH

Book Design
RON LIEBERMAN

ST. MARTIN'S PRESS NEW YORK

PRINTED IN SINGAPORE

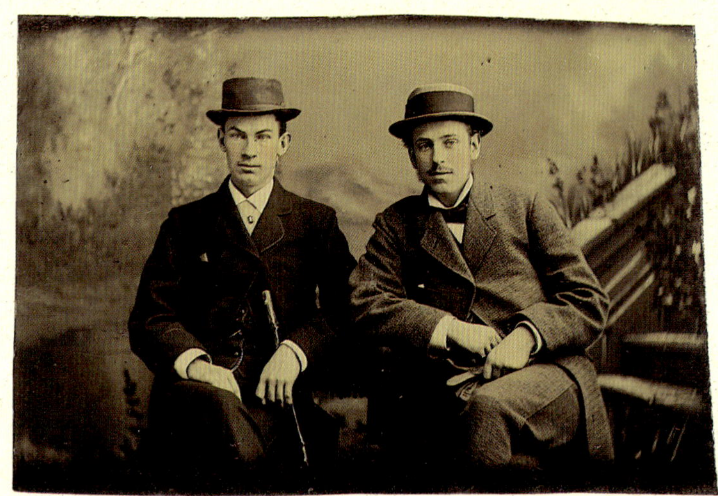

America c. 1860

Foreword

I FOUND LOVE ON A SUNDAY AFTERNOON. IT WAS THE KIND OF LAZY Indian summer afternoon that welcomed relaxation. I was in Pennsylvania, a favorite part of my world. Instead of lying in the shade with a good book as I usually do, I went to a flea market. All sorts of things turned my head that day, but I liked nothing enough to take home with me. As I went around the corner at the end of the last aisle of vendors' tables, I noticed a small tintype—a sort of photograph—of two men together. These men didn't resemble each other as brothers might, nor did their ages seem different enough to suggest they might be father and son. They stared out at me from their slightly rumpled sliver of metal and spoke to me in a wordless way that touched my heart. For fifty cents these two men became mine. I became hooked on this sort of *ménage-à-trois* and would indulge myself whenever two appropriate men presented themselves. But I'll always remember the first. I'm still in love.

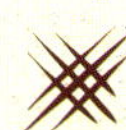

Unlike today, in nineteenth-century England and America, love between men was commonly expressed in a physical, though not necessarily a sexual, way. As the photographs in this book show, men walked together arm in arm and freely embraced. They talked and wrote romantically to each other. They danced together at "bull-dances." They slept together. Abraham Lincoln had a male friend with whom he shared a bed for almost four years. Thomas Edison chose the image of two men dancing as a fitting subject for one of his early moving picture experiments. Who could tell which of these affectionate men were sexual lovers? Who could be certain even about Walt Whitman, despite his immortalizing the "dear love of comrades" in *Leaves of Grass,* with such lines as:

For the one I love most lay sleeping by me under the same
    cover in the cool night,
In the stillness in the autumn moonbeams his face was
    inclined toward me,
And his arm lay lightly around my breast—and that night I
    was happy.

...two simple men I saw to-day on the pier in the midst of
    the crowd, parting the parting of dear friends,
The one to remain hung on the other's neck and passionately
    kiss'd him,
While the one to depart tightly prest the one to remain in
    his arms.

Even today some literary historians argue that although Whitman wrote explicitly about his feelings of love for a variety of men, he left no record of actual sexual consummations of these feelings.

By the end of the century, when Oscar Wilde was imprisoned for "the love that dare not speak its name," it was, in fact, not the voice of love but the voice of sexuality that was being silenced. Henceforth male-to-male love and male-to-male sex would be equally offensive in the eyes of society.

As a result of this change in attitude, throughout the twentieth century many men who loved other men lived suppressed lives, hiding behind the facade of wife and children. They were forced to live lies to avoid social ostracism. But many others rebelled, moved to large cities, and pursued what came to be known as the gay life. These rebels flaunted their love and their sexuality and started to become visible again. They began to integrate themselves into a world that is gradually coming to terms with their need for acceptance.

Some of the men pictured in this book may have been what we now consider gay; others assuredly were not. At the dawn of the twenty-first century, man's love for his fellow man is being reappraised. Perhaps the label *homosexual* will be discarded as obsolete, perhaps the word *gay* will once again just mean merry, and Whitman's "love of comrades" will prevail regardless of a man's chosen sexuality.

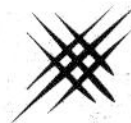

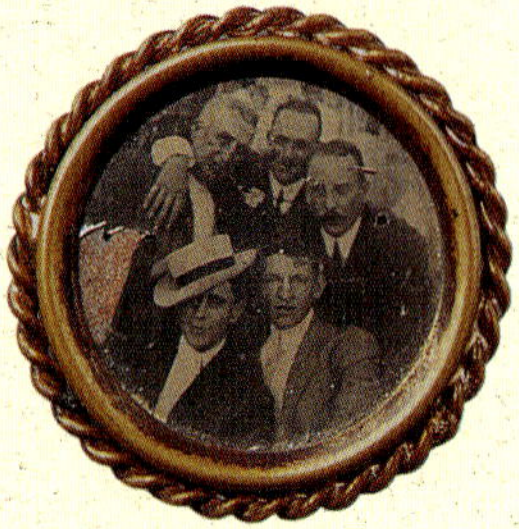

In 1839, the Frenchman Louis Jacques Mandé Daguerre's passion for experimentation led him to a new method of transferring a living image to an inanimate metal plate. These magical images, whose reflective mirrorlike surfaces needed to be held at just the right angle to be viewed clearly, were instantly popular when shown to the public. Delicate, they needed to be protected under glass, and later would be presented in hinged, embossed-leather or paper-covered wooden cases lined with velvet or satin. Within the year, the daguerreotype process reached New York and became a runaway success. Photographic studios proliferated, and photographic portraits became fashionable. The earliest image in this book is of the type that would immortalize Daguerre's name. It depicts two men, elegantly dressed in the style of 1848–50, sitting perfectly still while staring directly ahead. Their heads would have been supported with a contraption designed to keep them from moving during the long exposure to light necessary with this kind of early camera. Sometimes the sitters' faces would also need to be powdered white, in an effort to add enough brightness to make a successful exposure.

Though Daguerre achieved instant fame for his fascinating invention, another Frenchman, Joseph Nicéphore Niépce, actually gave the world its first permanent photographic image in 1826. He based his experiments on the *camera obscura*, an artist's aid that was used as early as 1500. At that time it would have been a darkened room, but Niépce used a darkened box with a small opening in one end which admitted light inside. On the opposite side of the box would appear an inverted image of what the camera saw. He inserted a treated metal plate into the box, exposing it to the view outside his window for eight hours.

The resulting photograph still exists today. Daguerre and Niépce became partners, but Niépce died in 1833, six years before Daguerre would announce the results of their experiments to the world.

The daguerreotype's popularity inspired others to experiment and produce different ways to capture images for all time. The ambrotype, which came in the same kind of decorative case as the daguerreotype, did not have its awkward reflective surface. It was a negative image on glass that appeared positive when backed with a dark background such as velvet. These images could be tinted to seem more lifelike. The ambrotype was introduced in 1854 and lasted until about 1865.

The tintype (or ferrotype), first made in 1856, followed the basic principle used in the making of the ambrotype, but the image was fixed on a thin sheet of iron (not tin) rather than glass. The backing was a dark varnish applied directly to the plate. Lightweight and virtually unbreakable, they were extremely popular during the Civil War—a soldier could now always carry a lifelike remembrance of his beloved with him or send an image of himself to someone far away. The tintype was inexpensive to produce and brought the miracle of photography to the masses. Millions were made. Traveling tintypists toured the country, snapping their subjects wherever they might be. Waiting time for the finished product could be as little as ten minutes. They would become popular at carnivals and tourist sites, where painted backdrops and other props could be used to mimic the photographer's studio or the local scenery. Tintypes (and also daguerreotypes) were mounted into jewelry. One could have a tiny portrait inserted into a ring, a pin, or even cuff links. Tintypes continued to be made into the twentieth century.

At the same time that Niépce and Daguerre were working in France, William Henry Fox Talbot was experimenting in England. As early as 1835, he produced images on paper. Unlike the previously described processes, which produced one-of-a-kind images from each exposure, Talbot's discovery could produce multiple prints from a negative resulting from one exposure. He gave us the basic method of photography still used today.

The world soon caught on to the various innovations possible with photographs produced on paper. The popular *carte-de-visite* was a mounted calling-card print that was fashionable from the mid-1850's through the 1870's but lasted until just after the turn of the century.

The cabinet card was a larger-sized, mounted paper print. It was often stamped with the photographer's name and address, which aids those of us who search for the history behind a particularly interesting image. Unlike daguerreotypes, ambrotypes, and tintypes, paper images can often be found with inscriptions by the previous owners, which are sometimes more amusing and provocative than the actual photograph itself. The larger size of the cabinet card allowed for the use of elaborate backgrounds and props. In fact, some collectors are only interested in collecting prints because of the background imagery.

In 1888, George Eastman introduced the Kodak camera. It soon became possible for virtually anyone to own one and to take pictures of any desired subject. The early Kodak cameras came loaded from the factory and could be used to take one hundred exposures. They needed to be returned to Kodak, processed, reloaded with film, then returned to the owner to be used again. In later years, Kodak encouraged its amateur photographers by printing postcards from their negatives. Soon photo postcards became so popular that some of these amateurs could turn professional and set up businesses at resorts, amusement parks, and elsewhere to profit from the public's mania for being photographed. Photo postcards can be dated from as early as the turn of the century and were still being made in 1939.

The camera became a staple of the average household, as did the snapshots it produced. Film could be bought, processed, and printed in every town across America and throughout the civilized world. By 1947, the amazing new Polaroid camera could produce a truly instant photograph in sixty seconds. Color transparency film became available in 1935 but did not compete with the popularity of the black-and-white snapshot until the 1960's.

The photographs shown in this book are examples of the portrait photographer's art as described above. I choose not to collect prints from color negatives as they seem too recent and are less interesting to me than the subtle, toned images that resulted from the discoveries of Daguerre, Talbot, and their contemporaries. What you see here represents about one third of my collection and, of course, those images that I consider the best. This book is an homage to an affection that has endured and will endure for all time—a record of the emotional closeness of men, regardless of their sexuality. It is a celebration of a man's love for his chosen comrade.

New York City,
March 1998

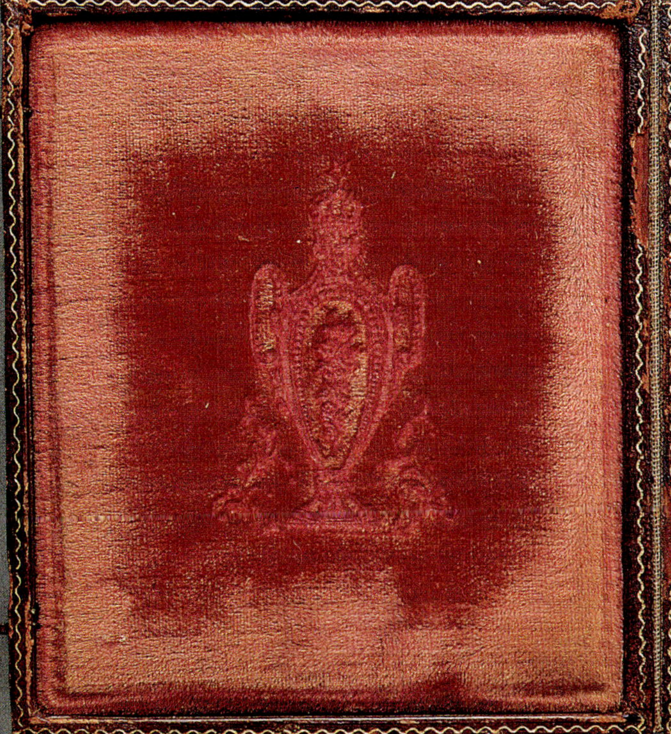

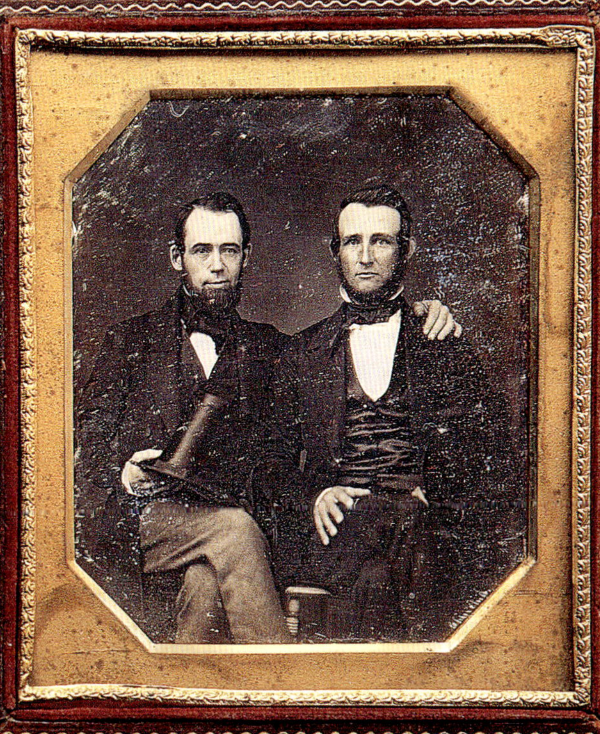

America 1848–50

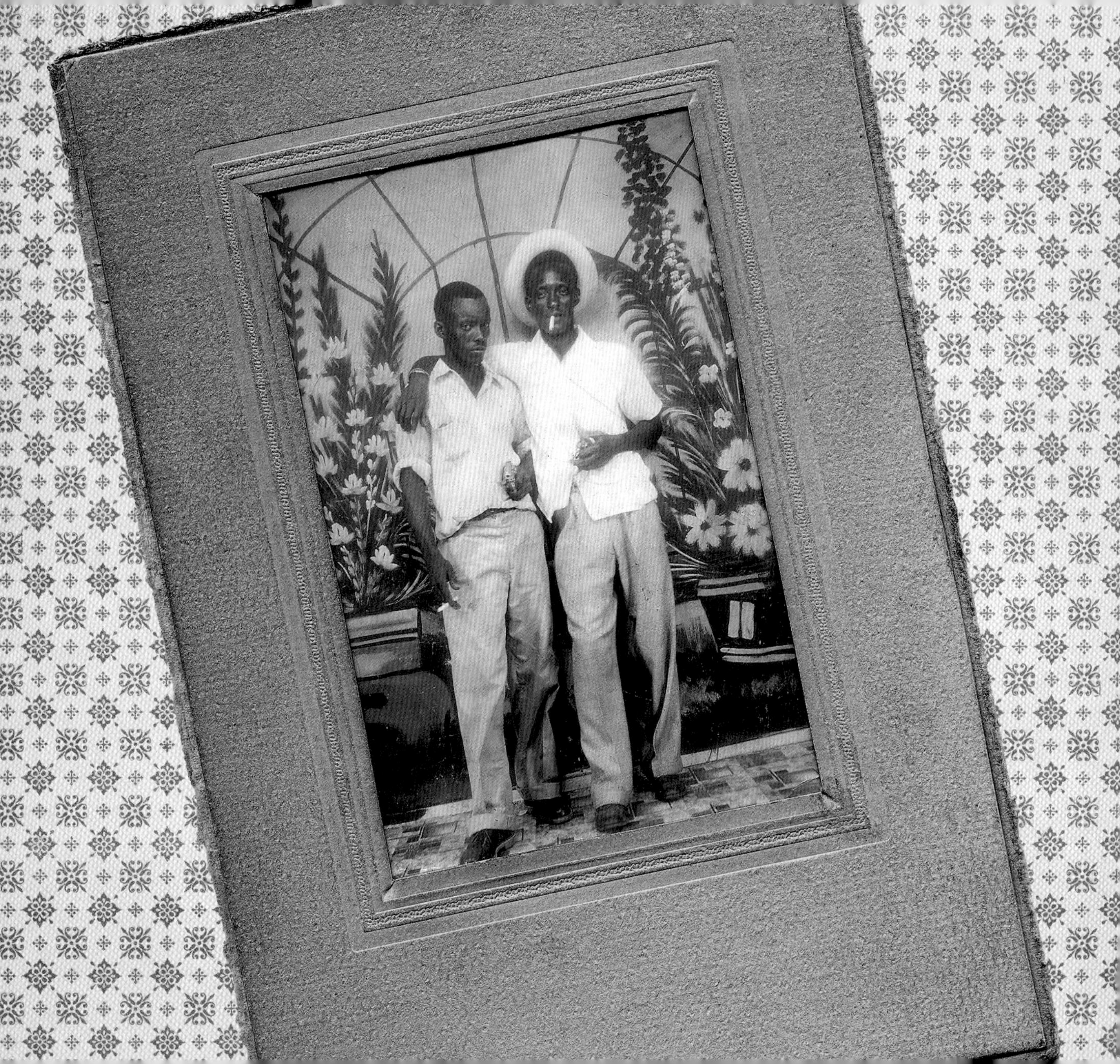

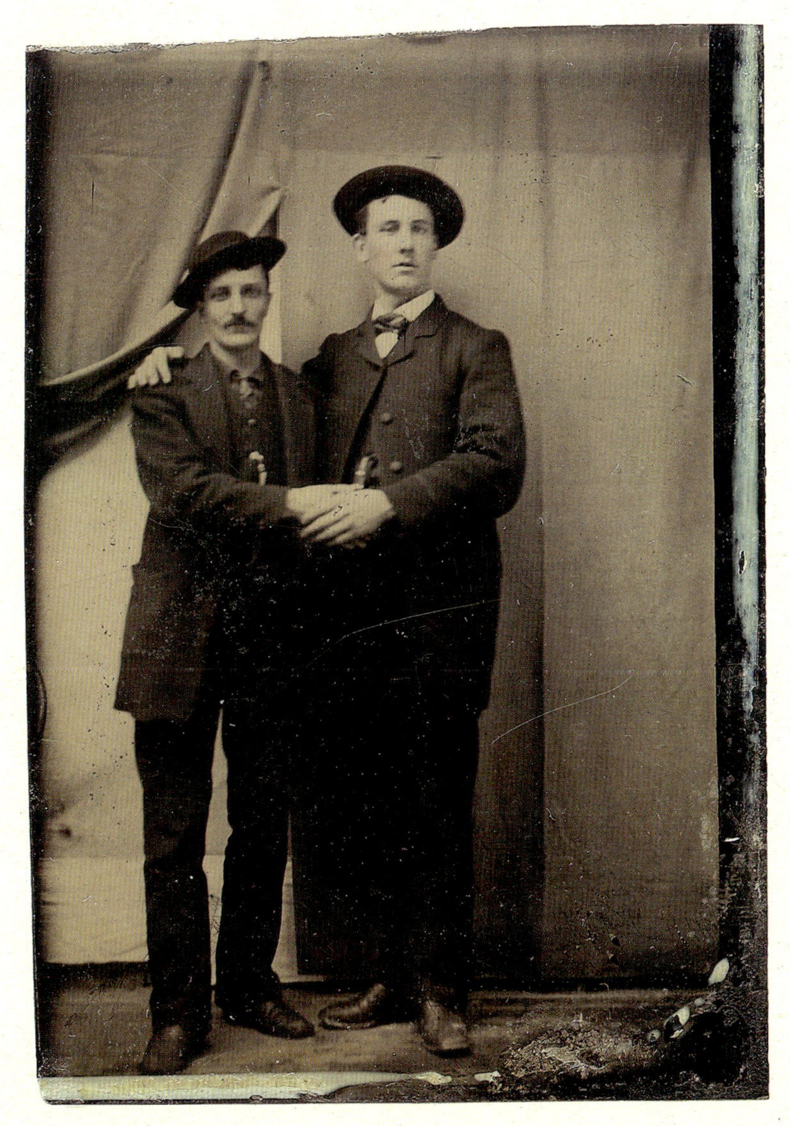

America 1880's
➤ *America 1935–40*

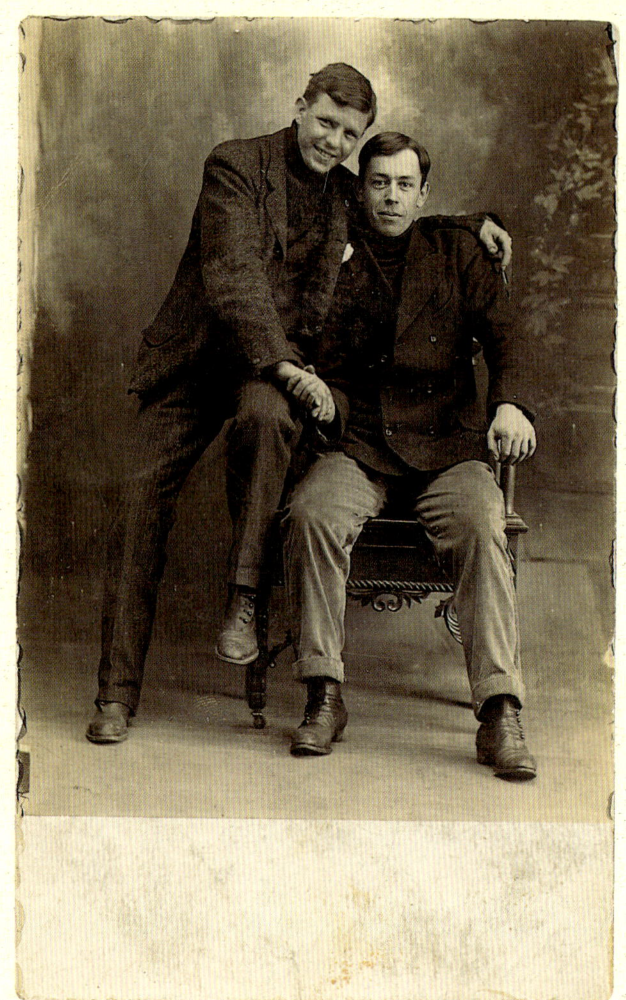

America c. 1905

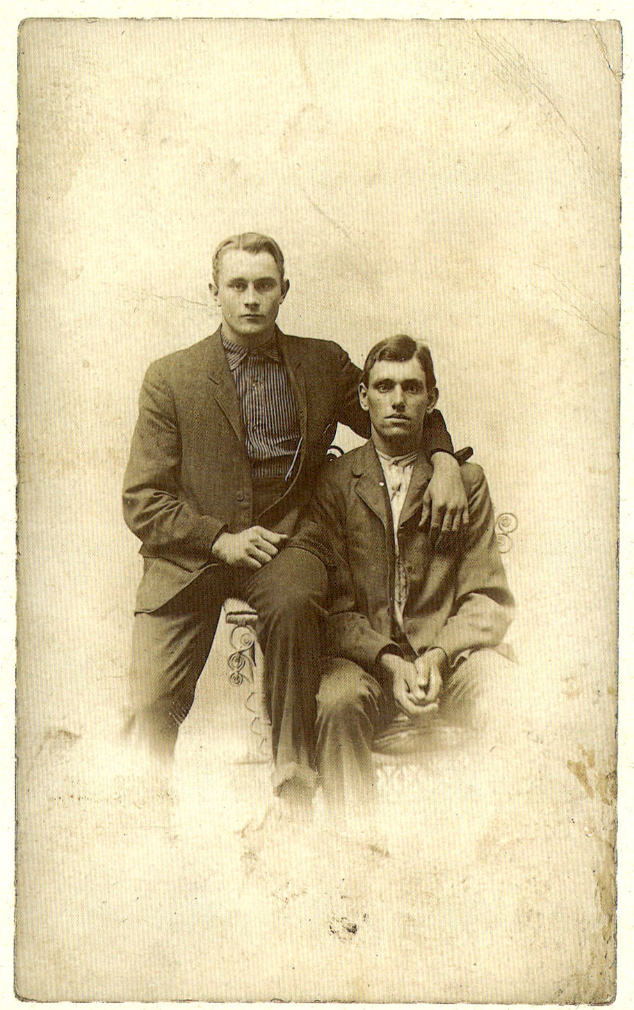

America 1901–06

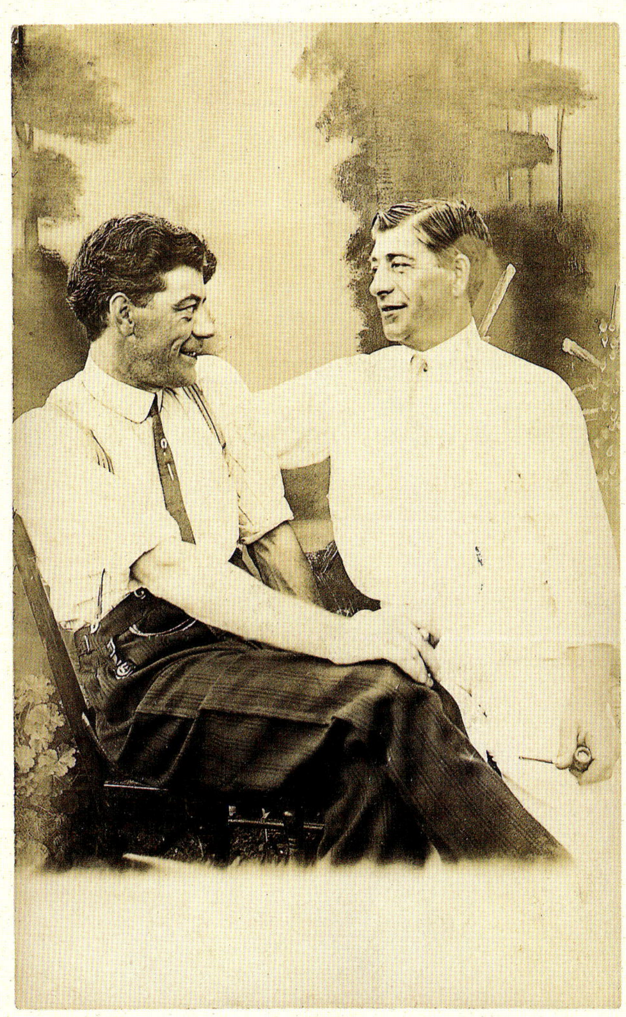

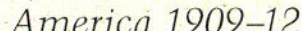

America 1909–12

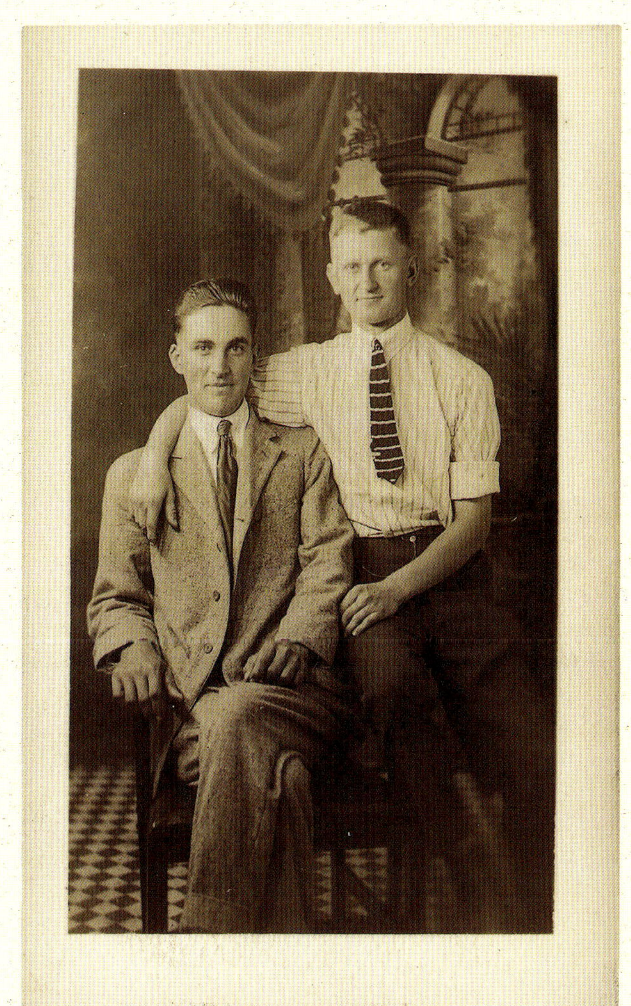

America mid-1920's

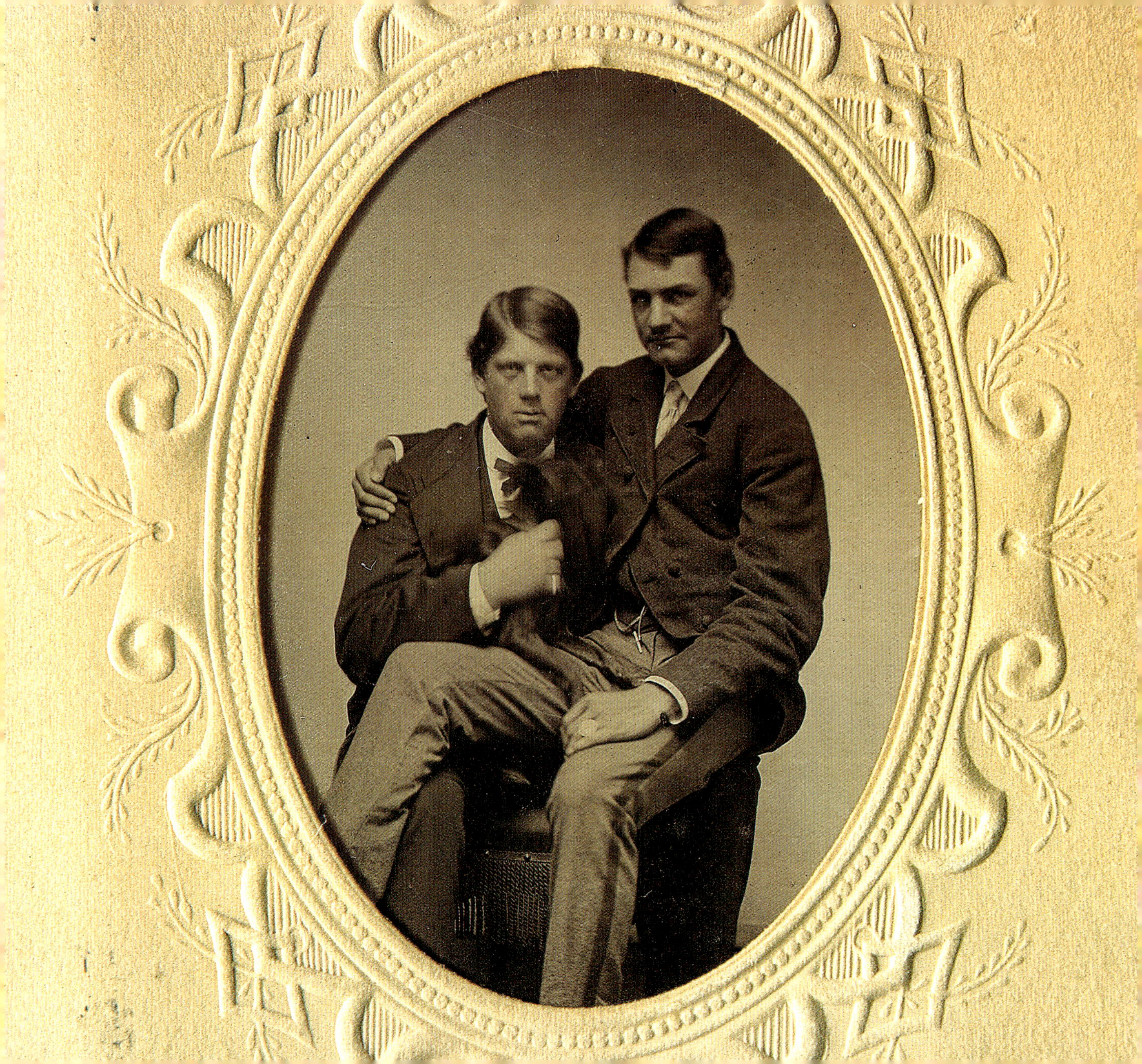

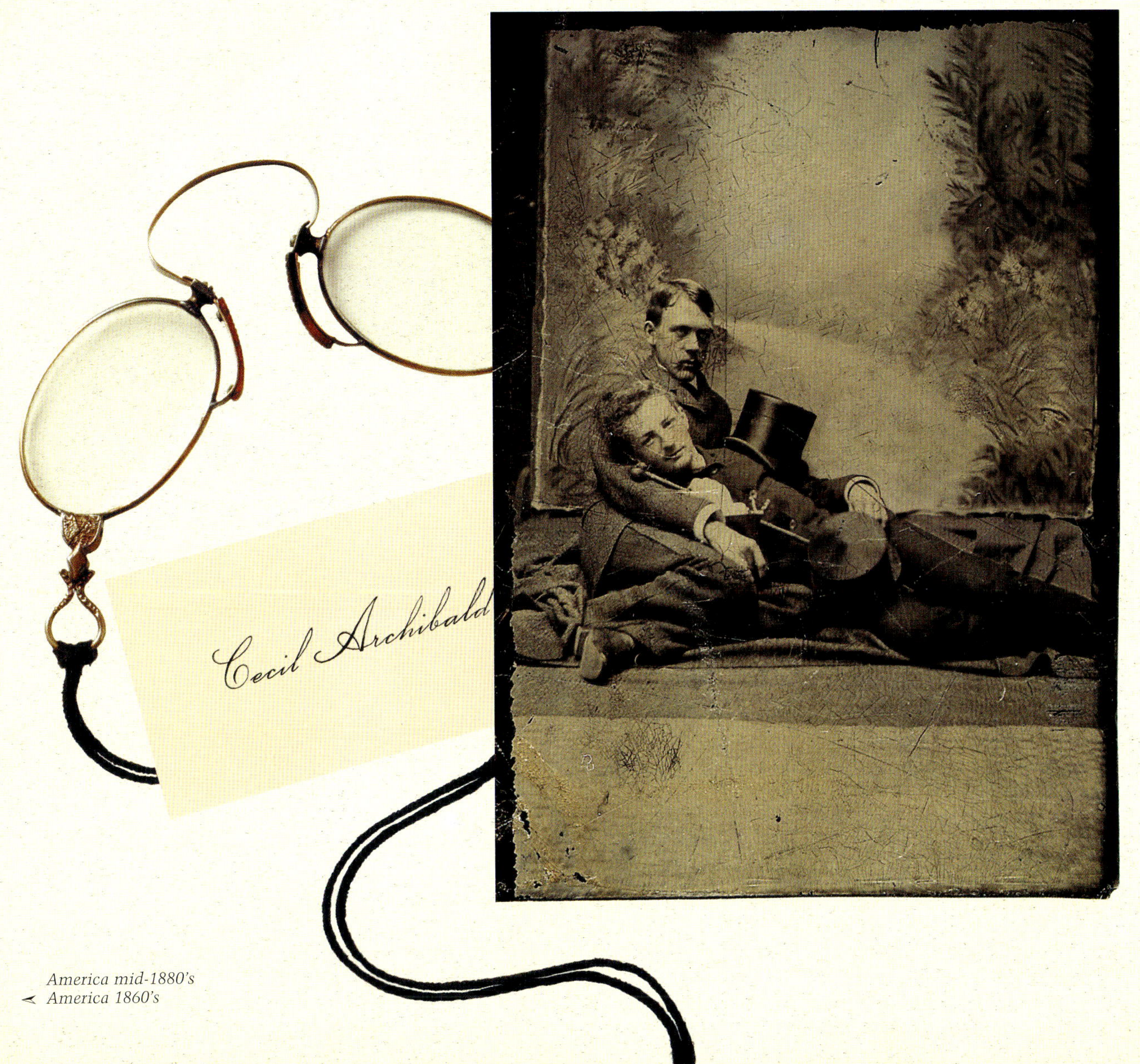

America mid-1880's
◄ America 1860's

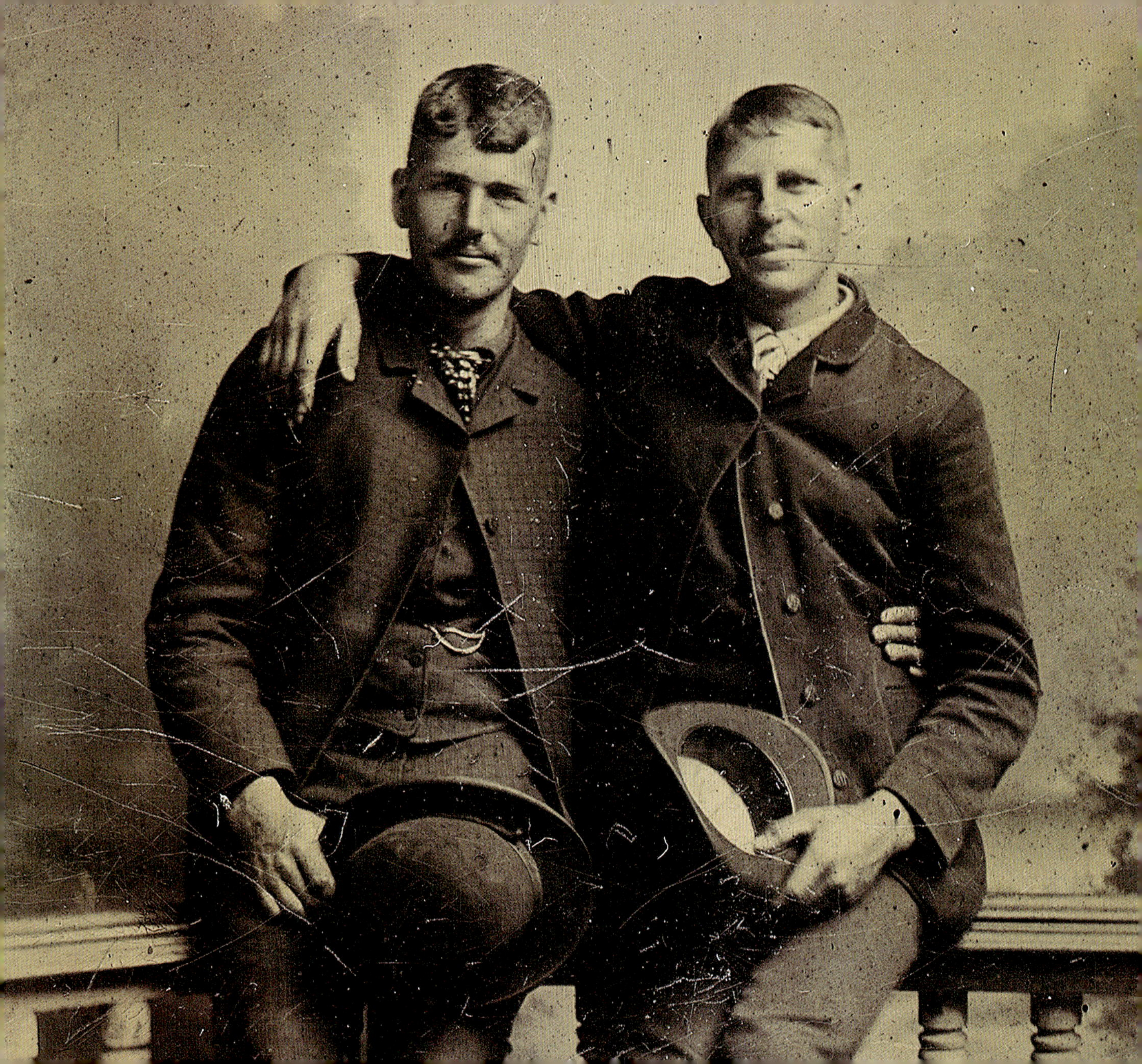

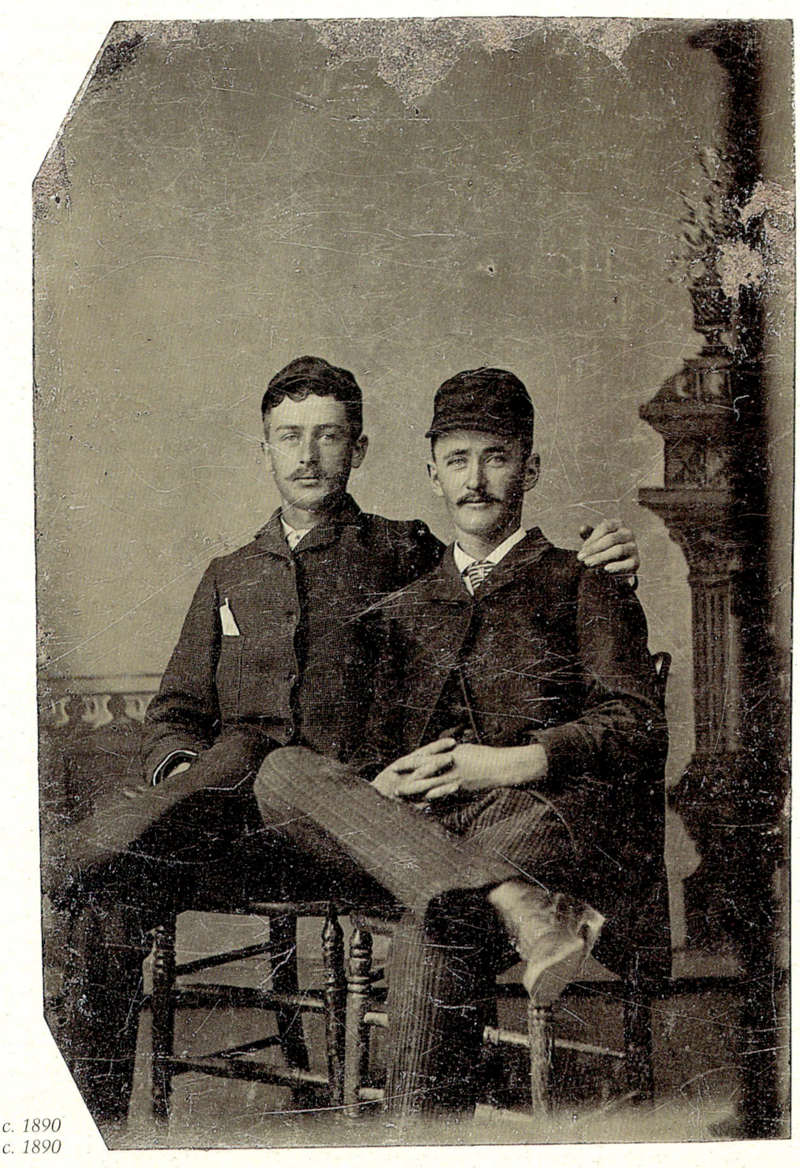

America c. 1890

➤ America c. 1890

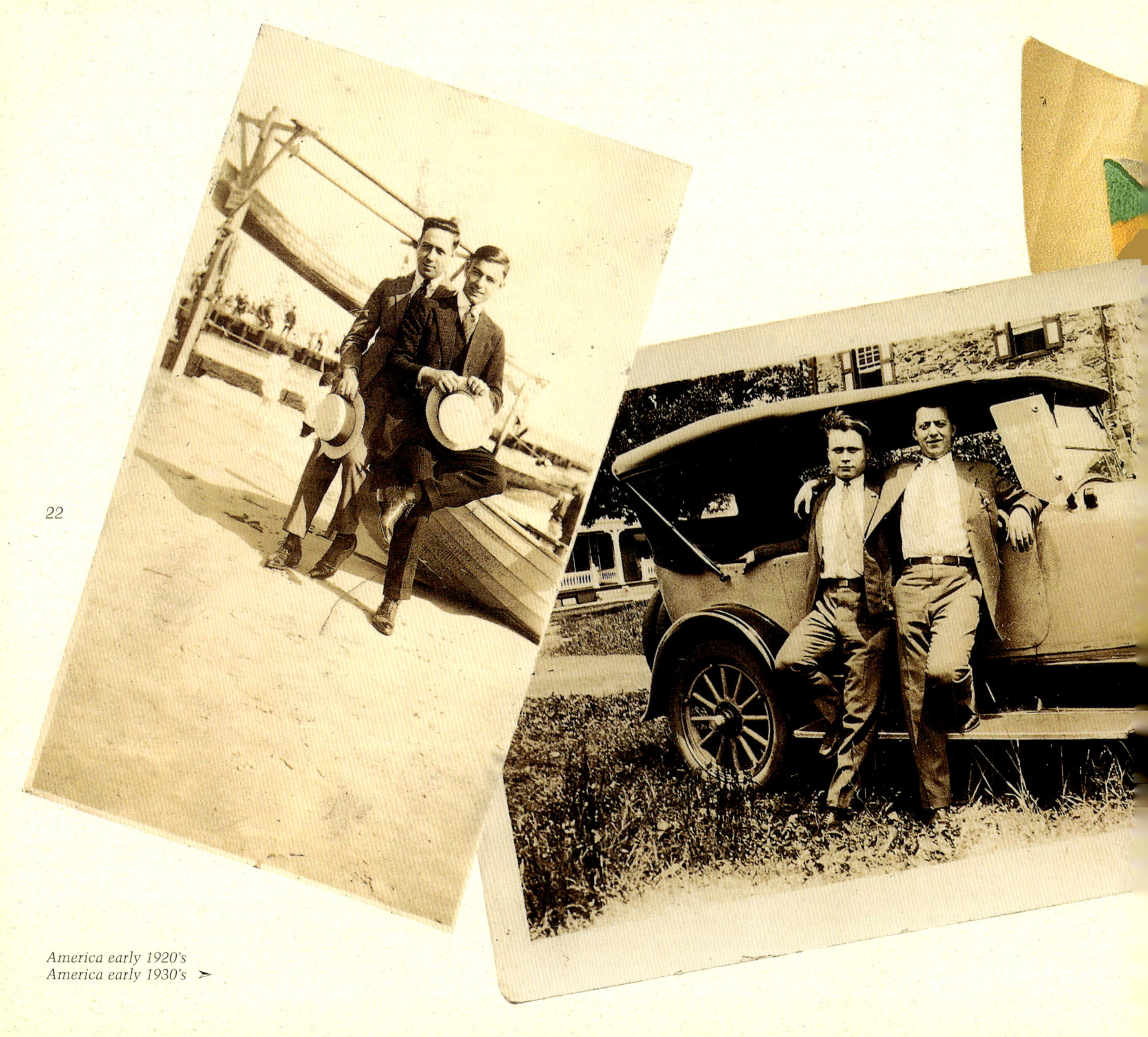

America early 1920's
America early 1930's ➢

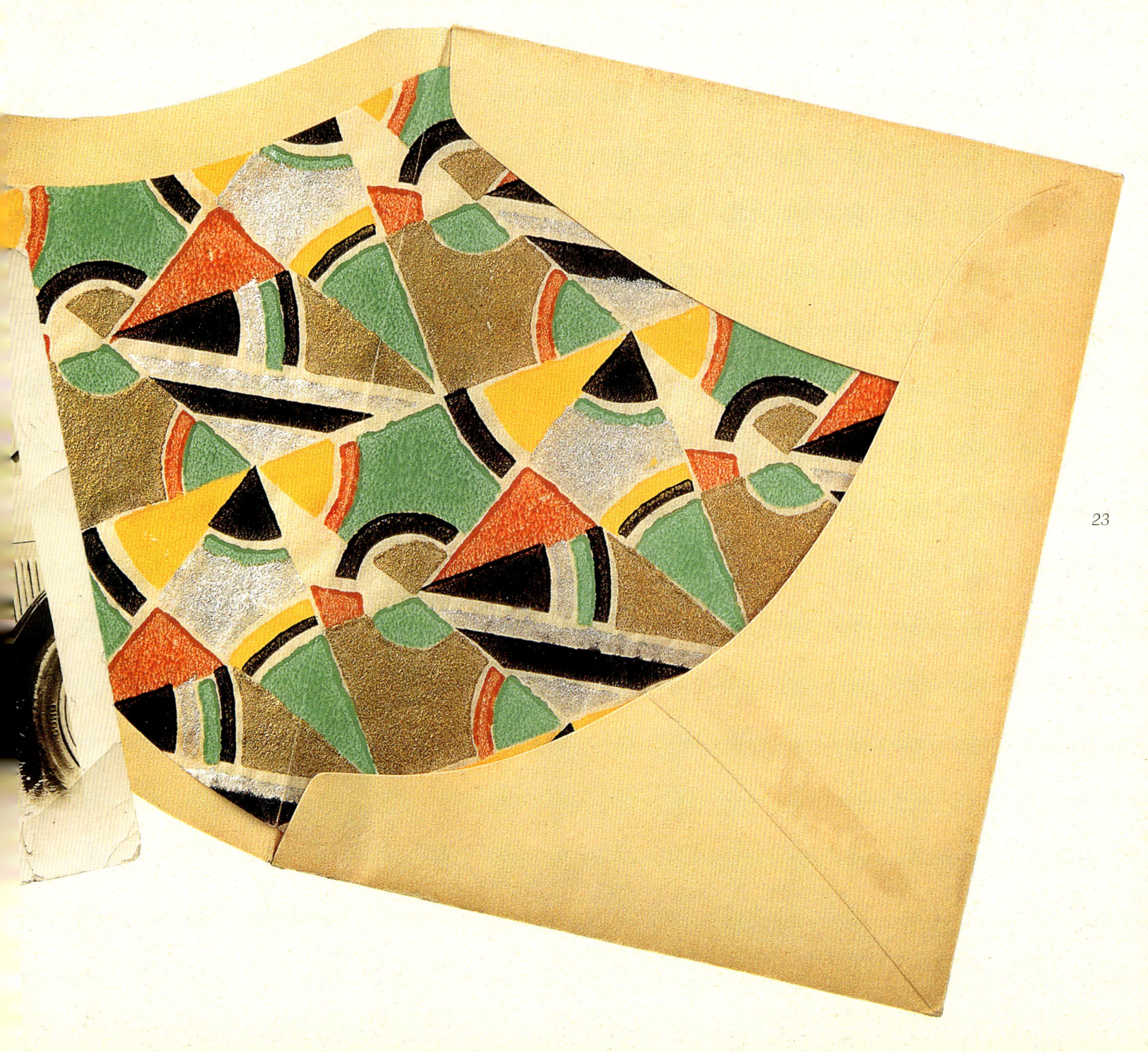

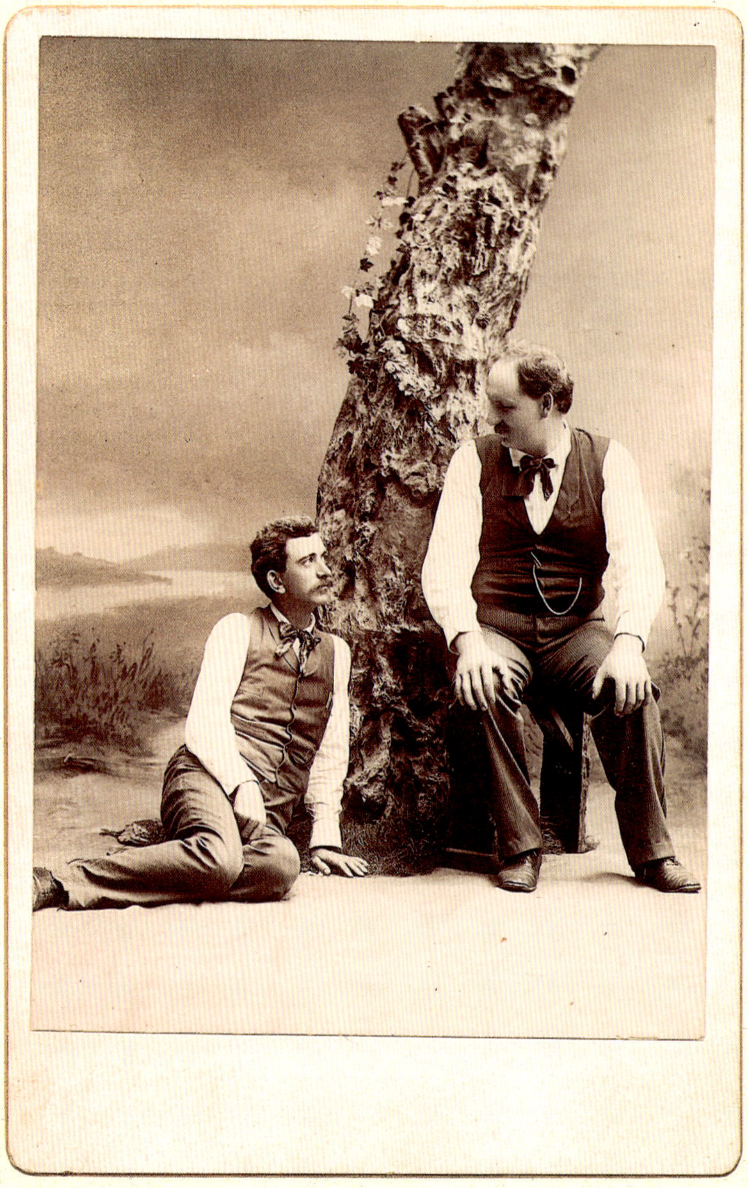

America c. 1890
America 1915 ➢

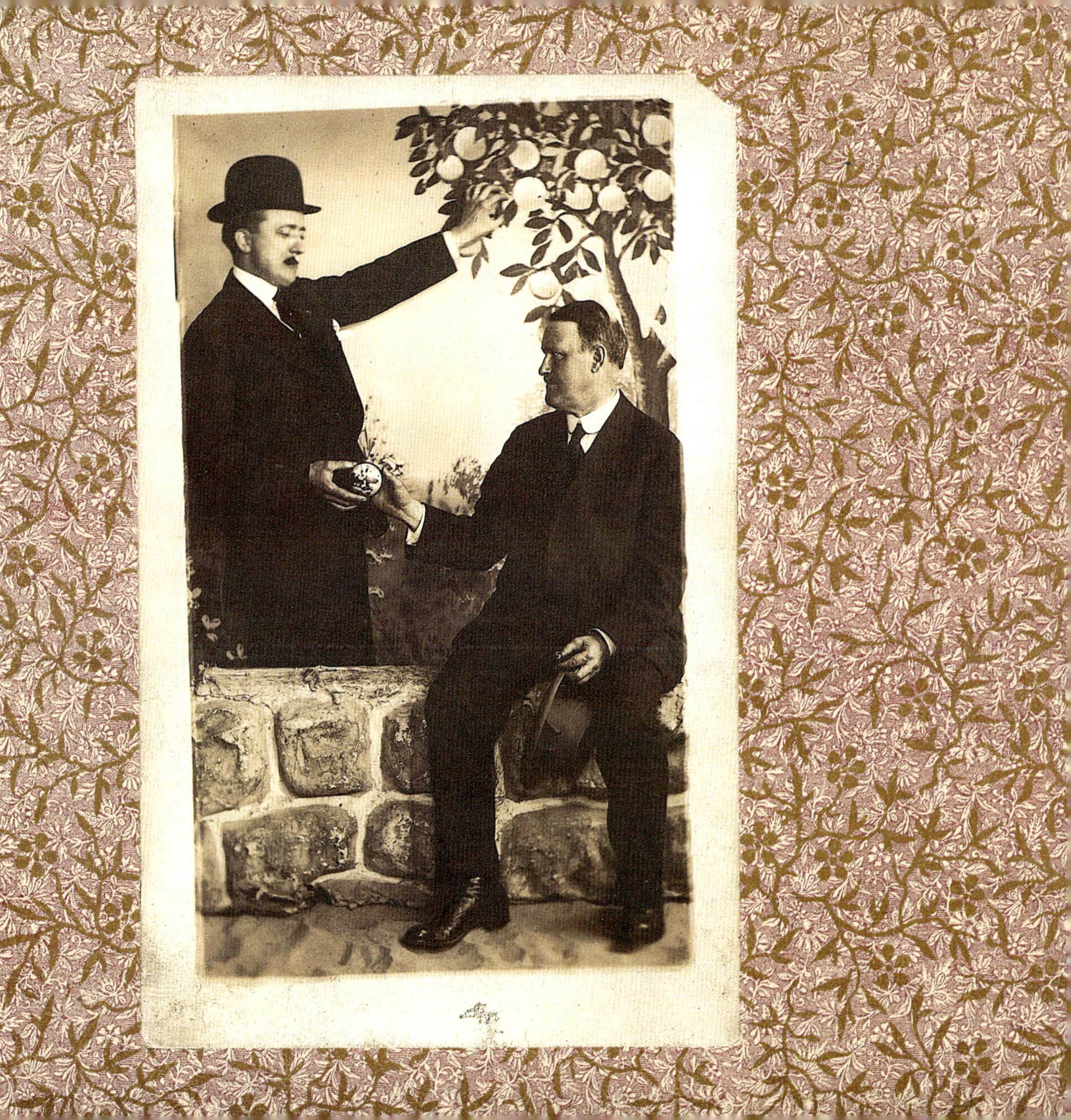

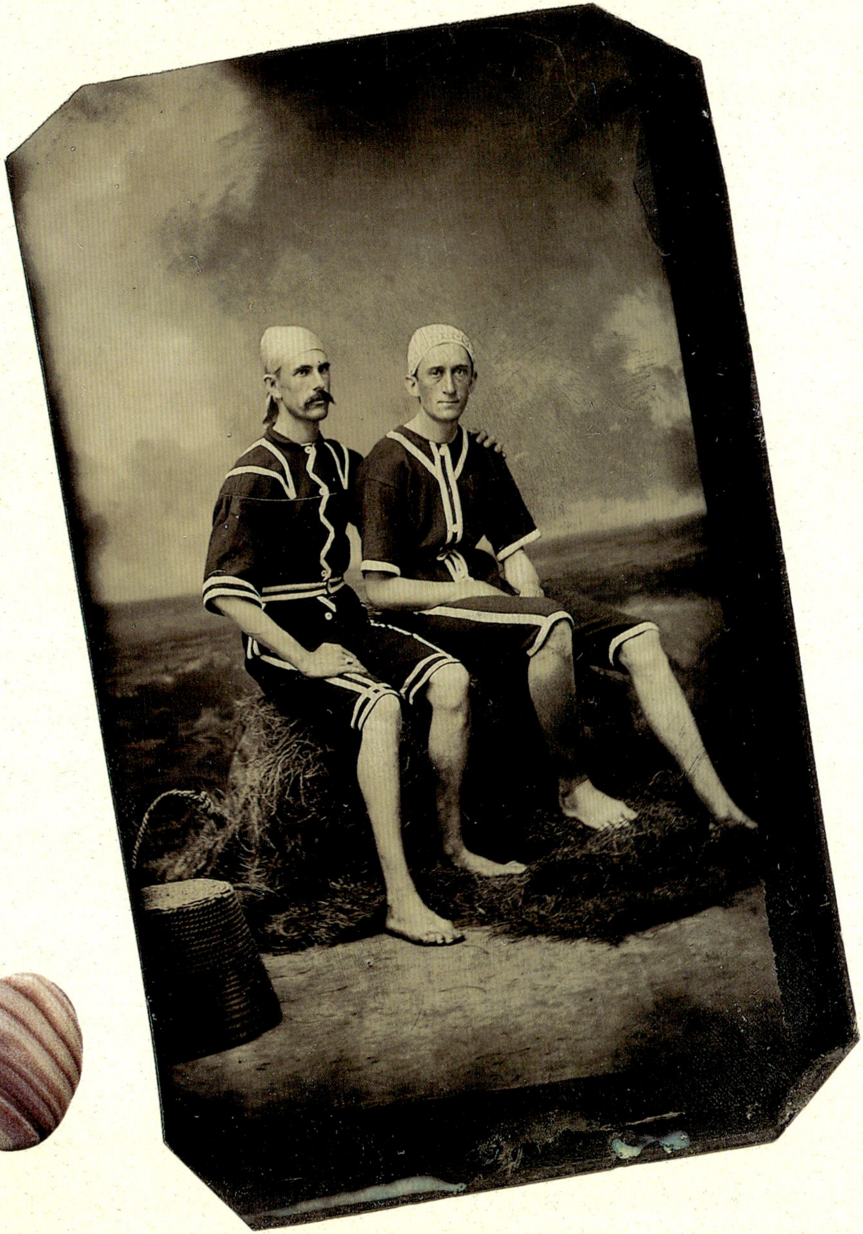

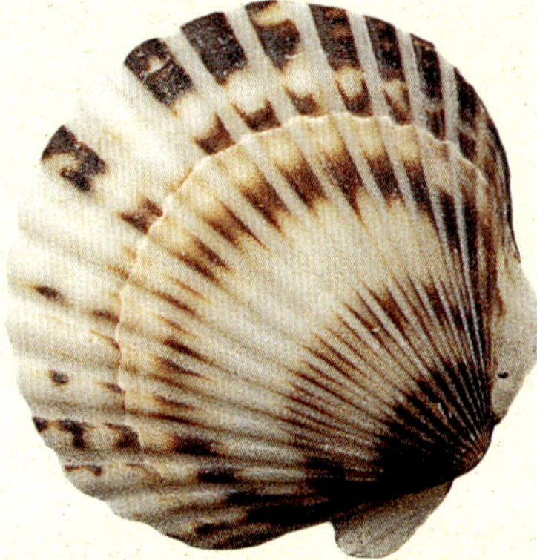

America c. 1885
Germany 1913 ➢
America c. 1885 ➢

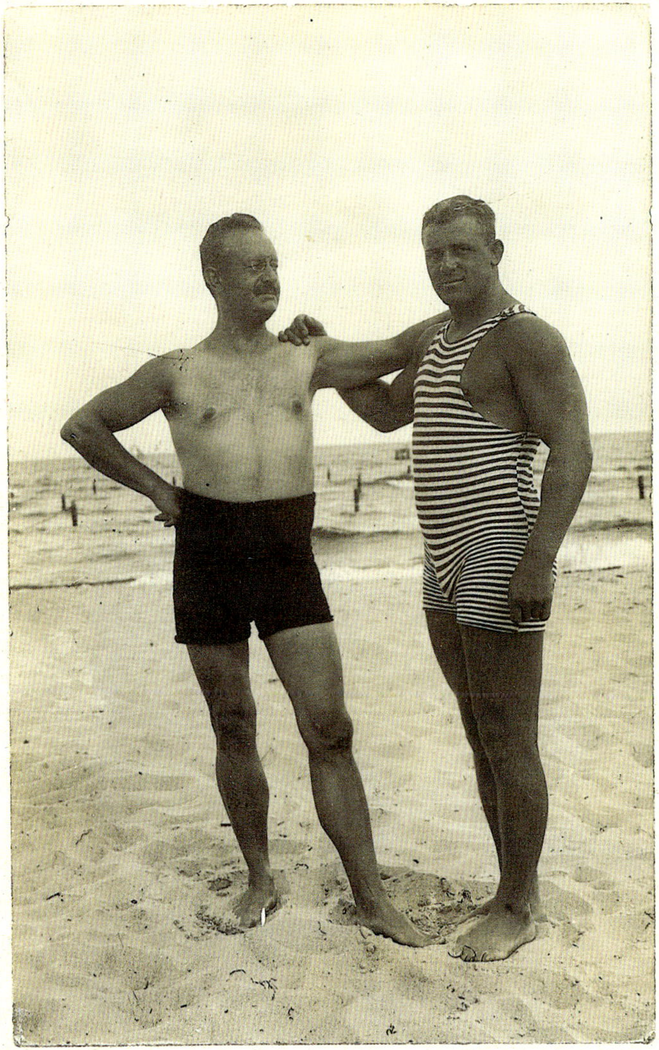

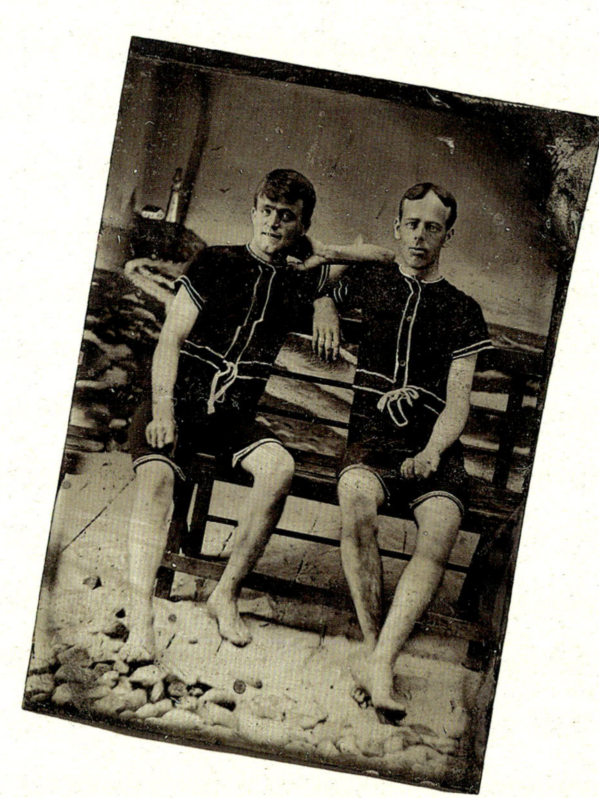

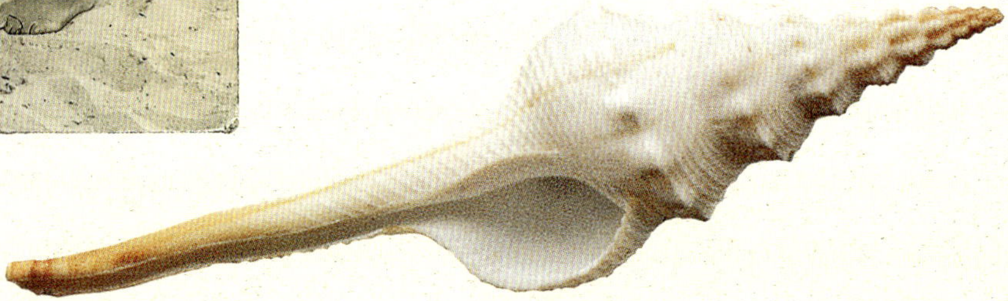

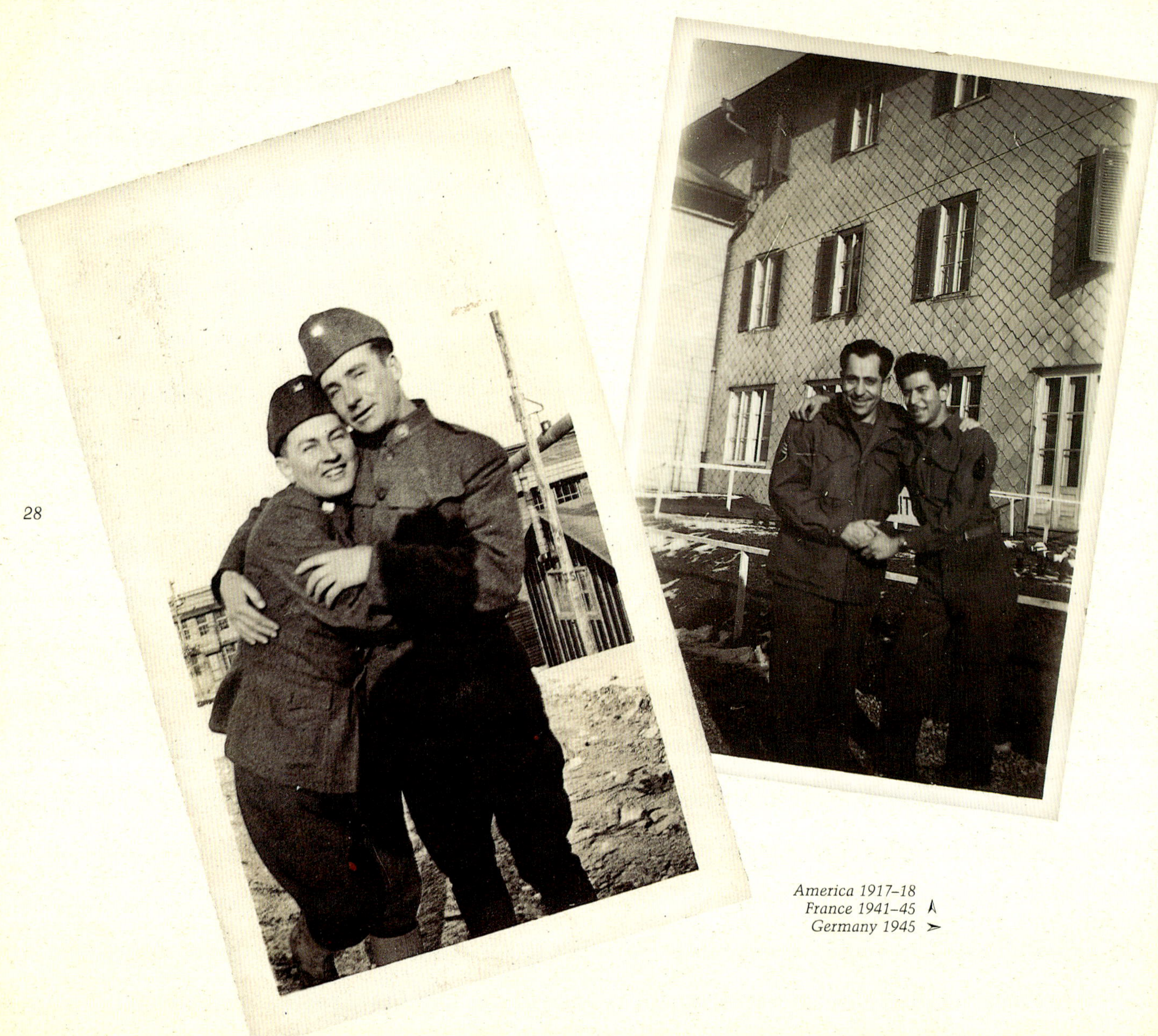

America 1917–18
France 1941–45 ⋏
Germany 1945 ➢

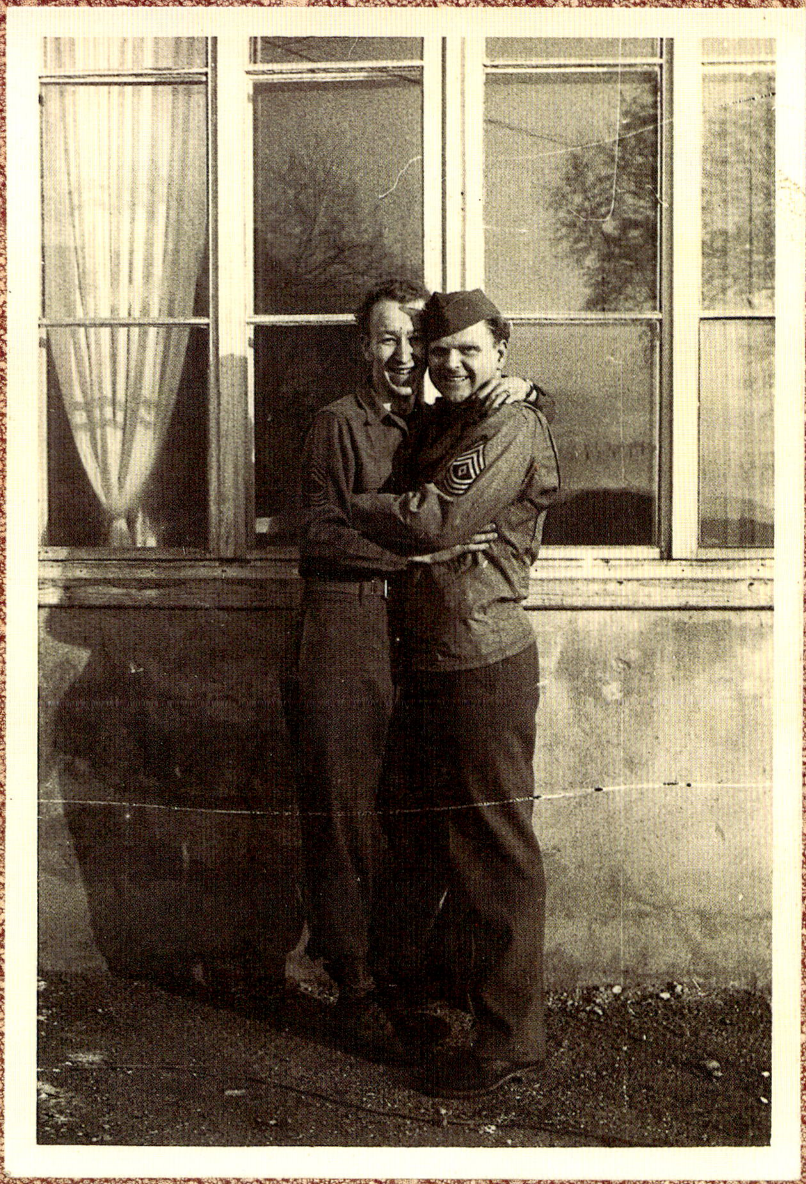

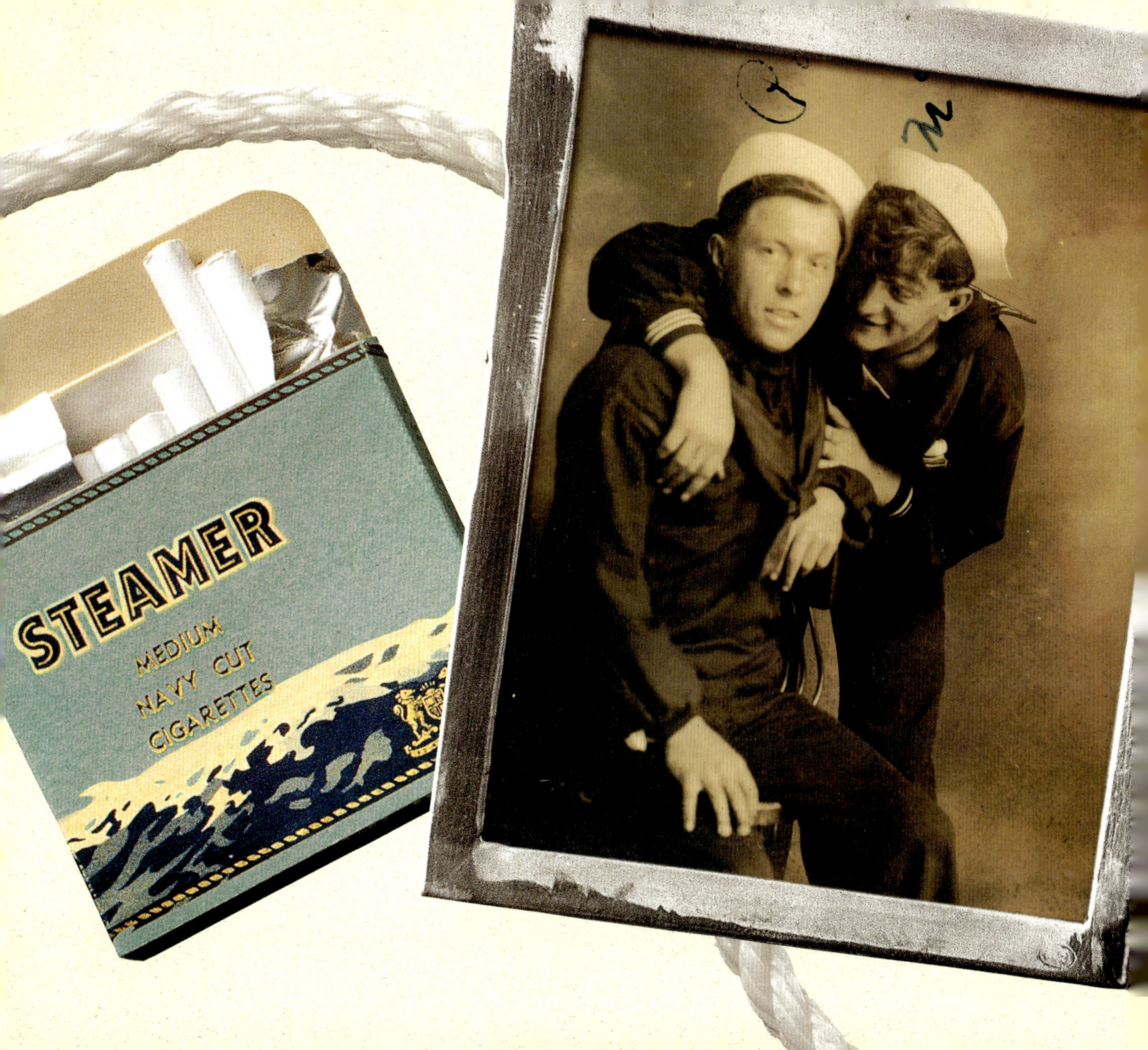
STEAMER
MEDIUM
NAVY CUT
CIGARETTES

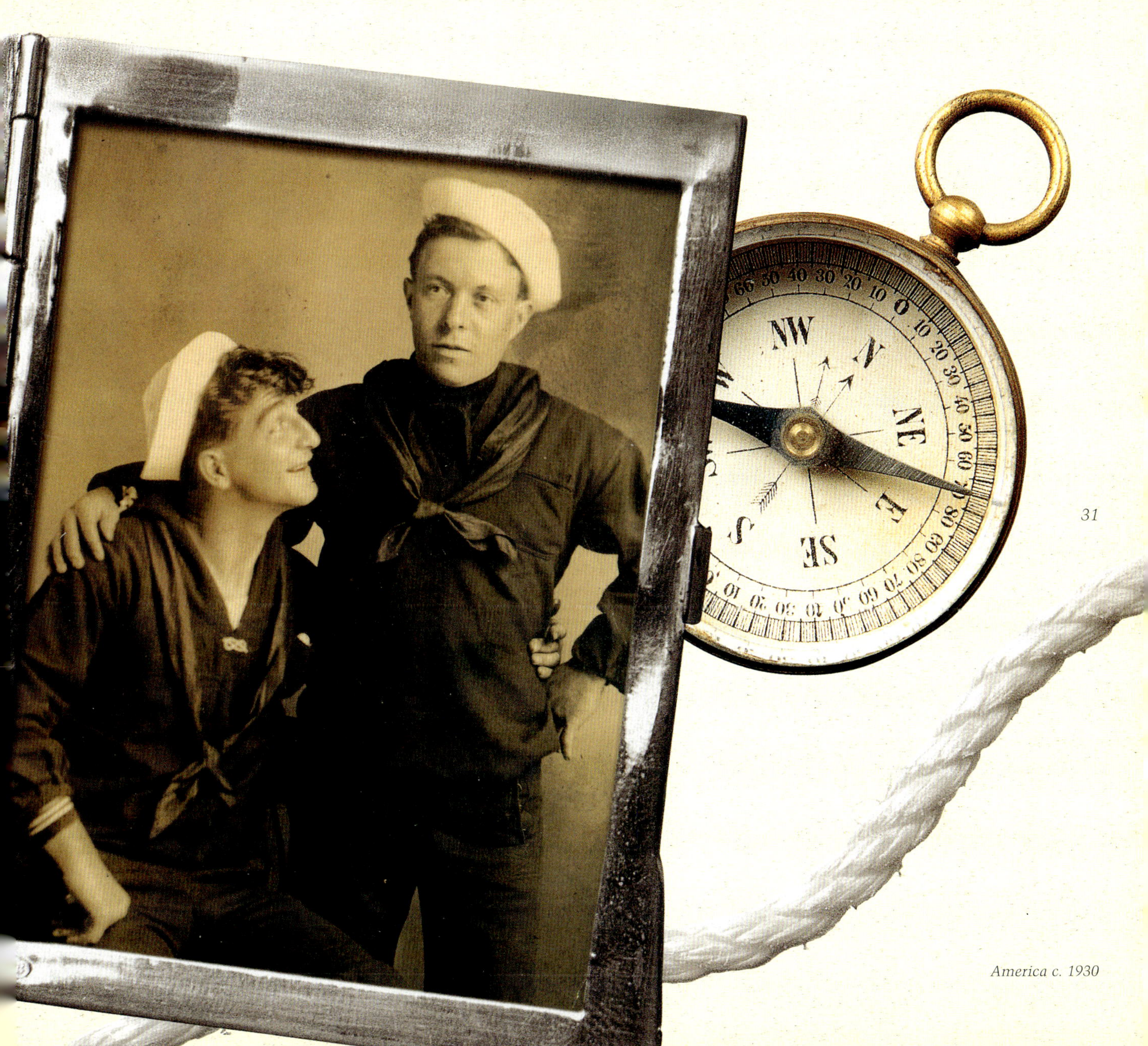

America c. 1930

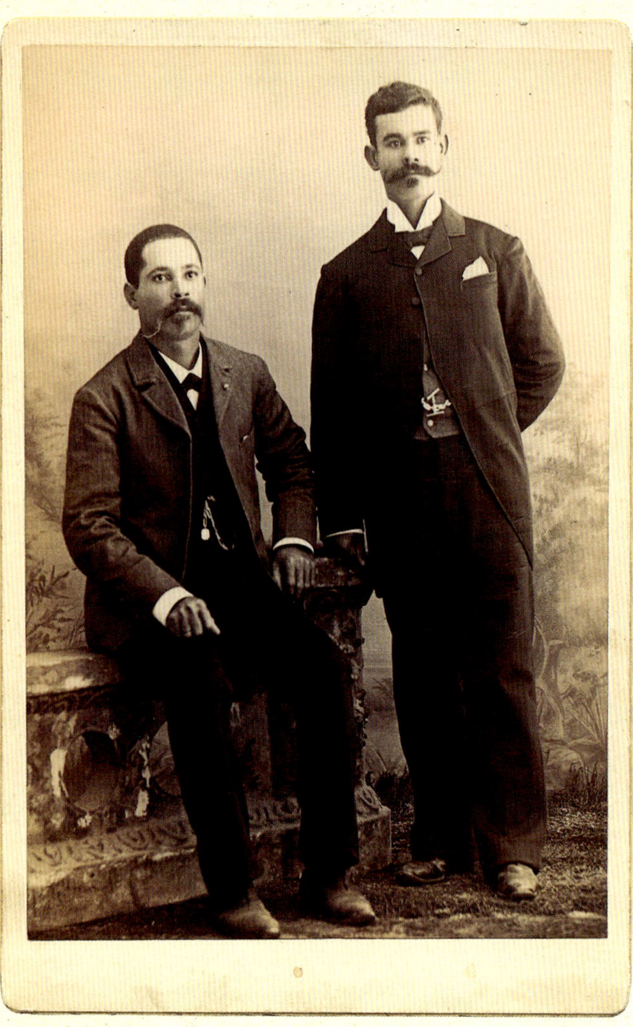

West Indies 1896

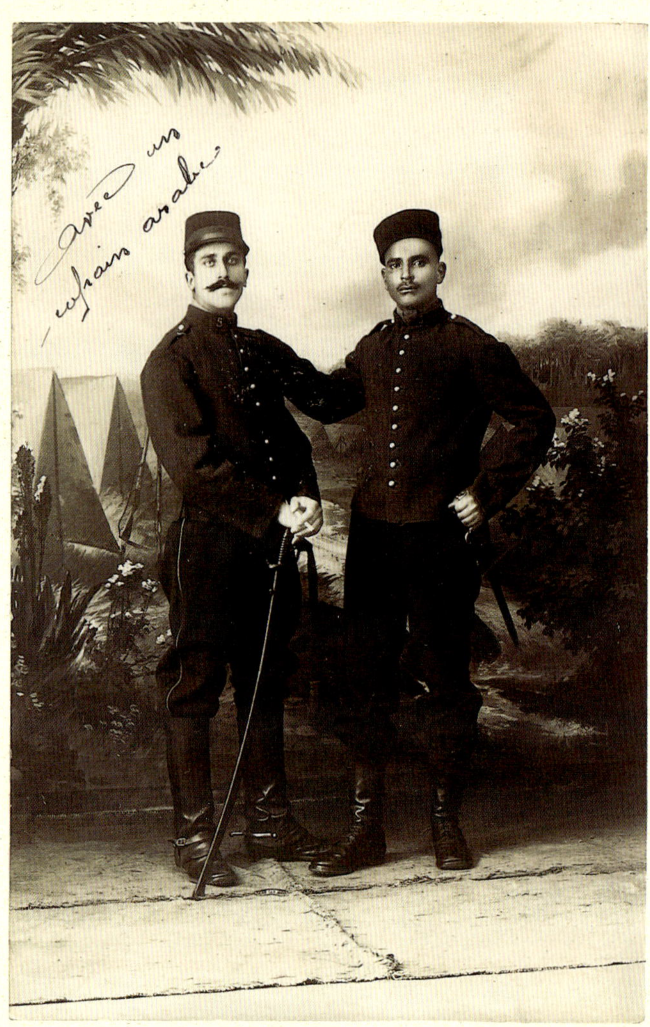

France 1912

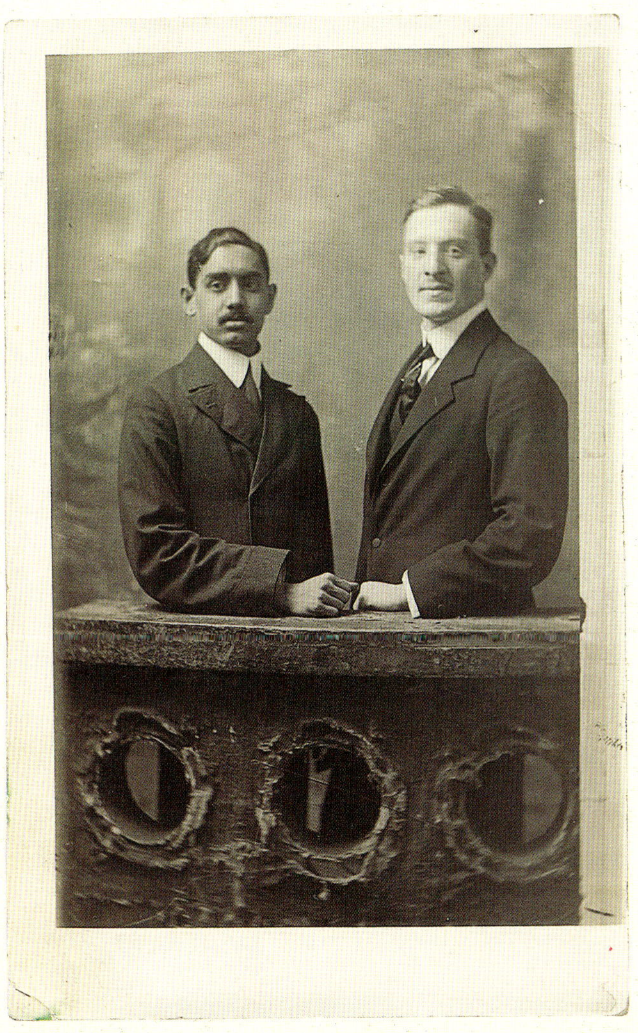

England 1910

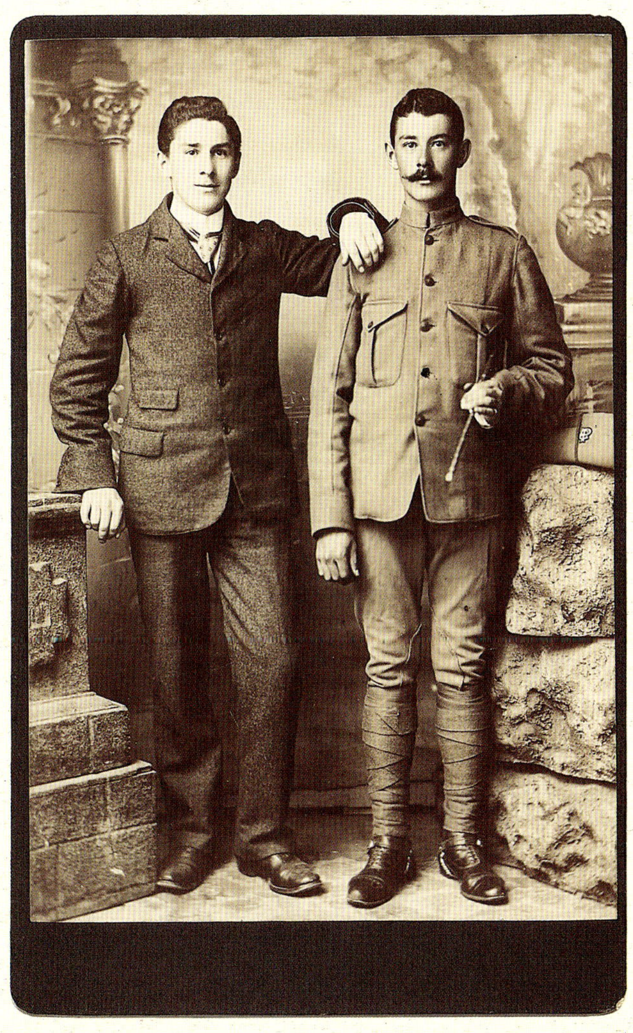

South Africa 1914–18

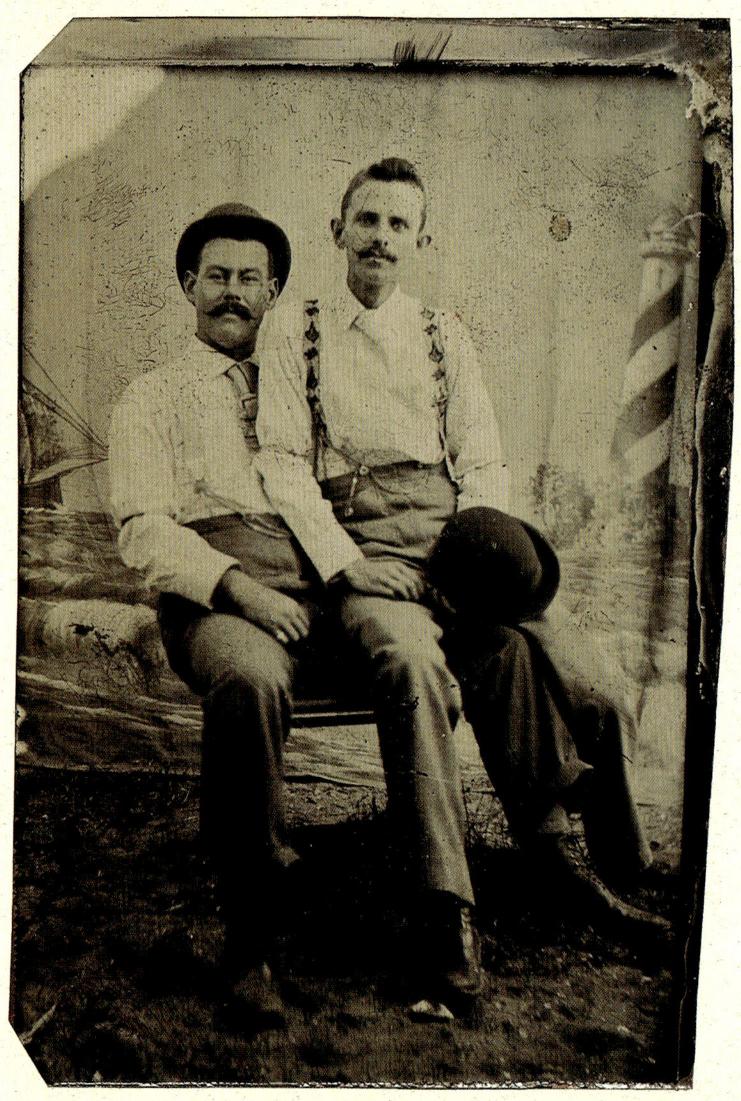

America 1880's
America 1880's ➢

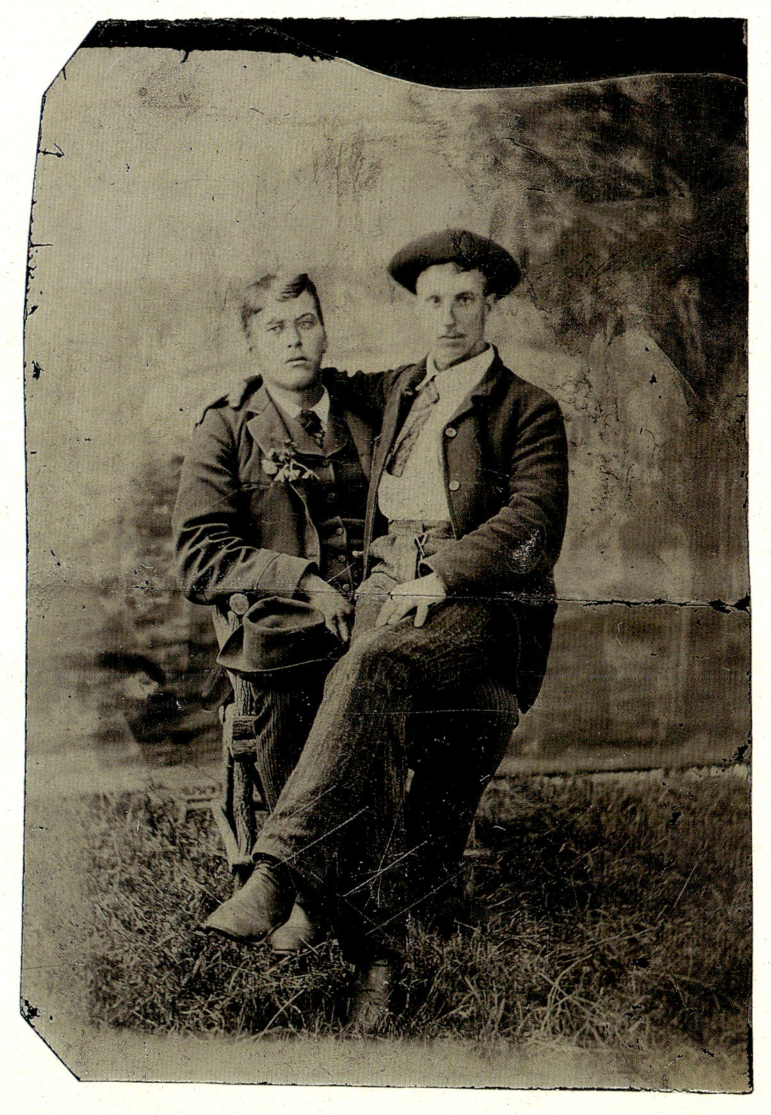

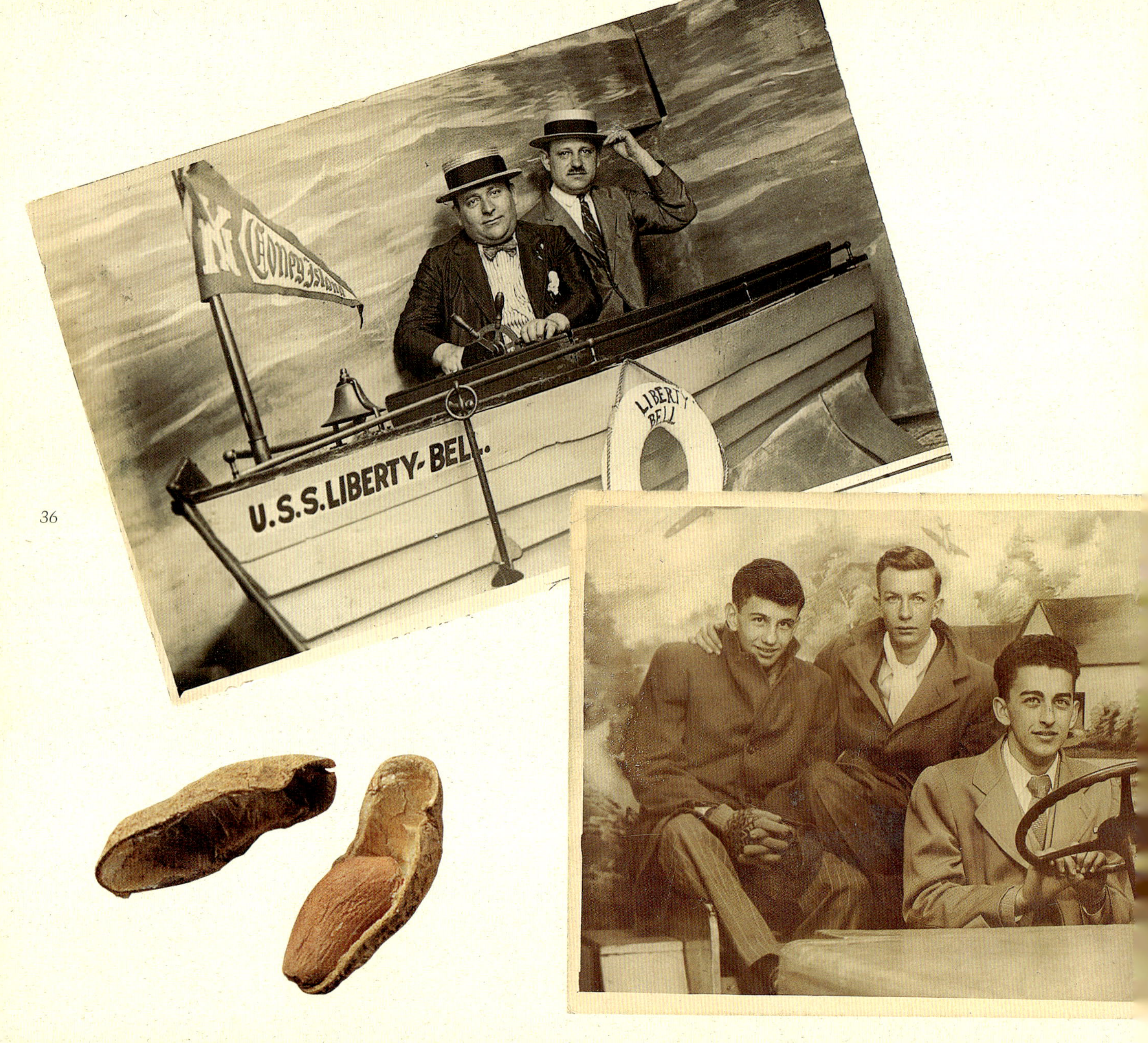

NY Coney Island
LIBERTY BELL
U.S.S. LIBERTY-BELL

America 1951
➤ America c. 1940
➤ America c. 1945

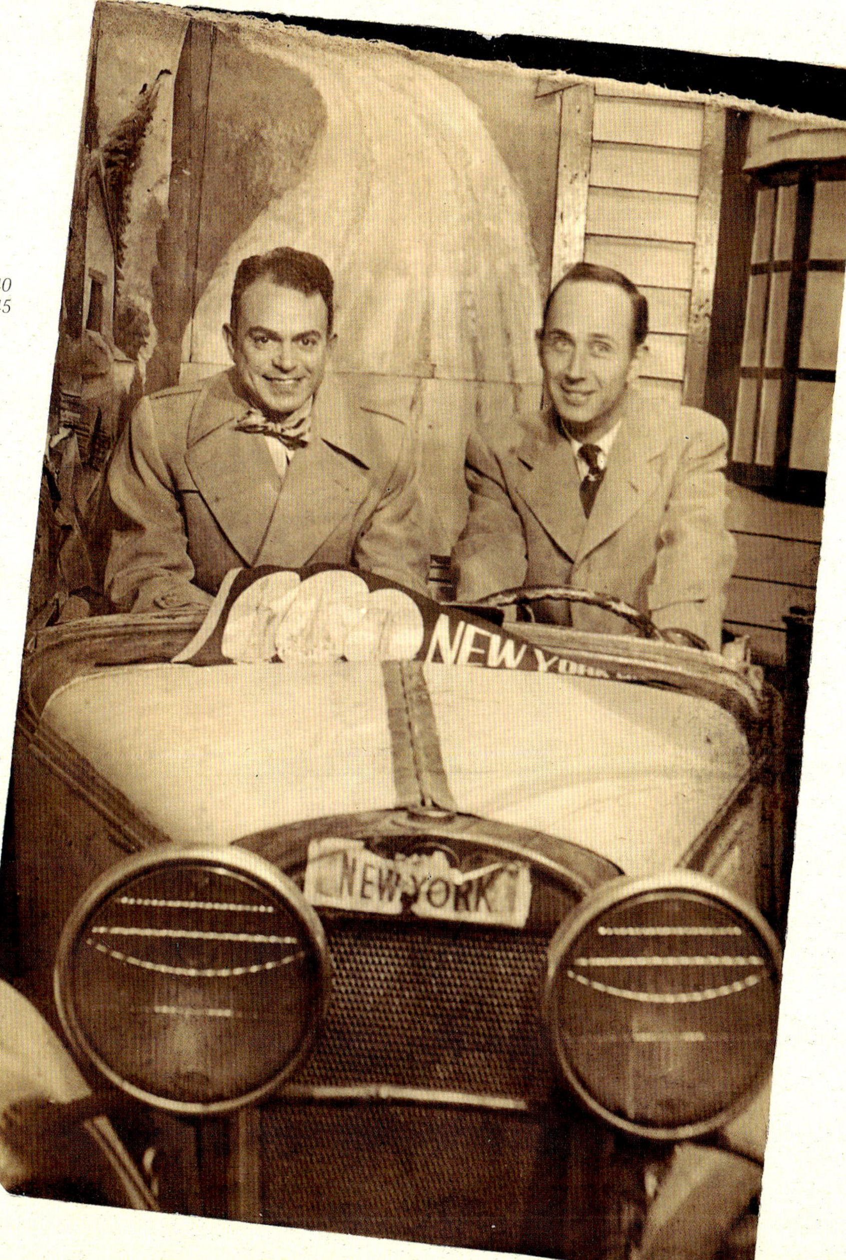

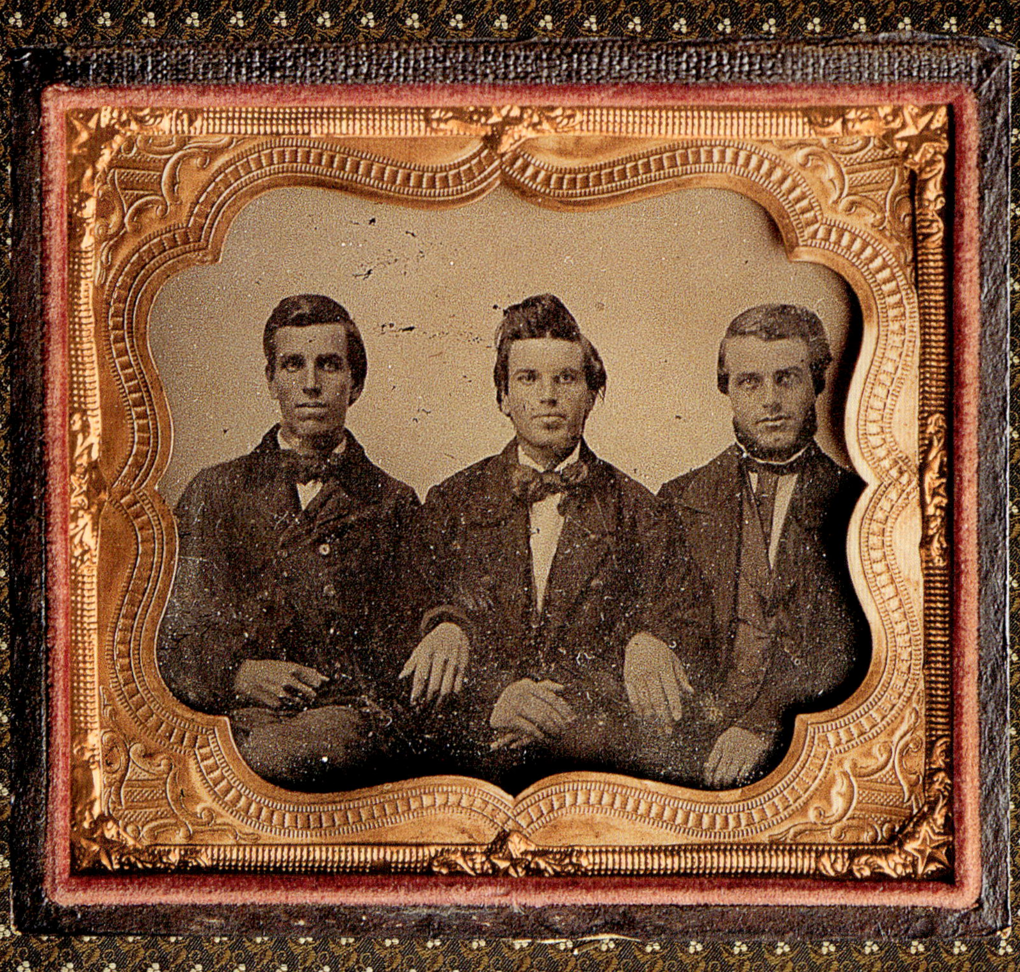

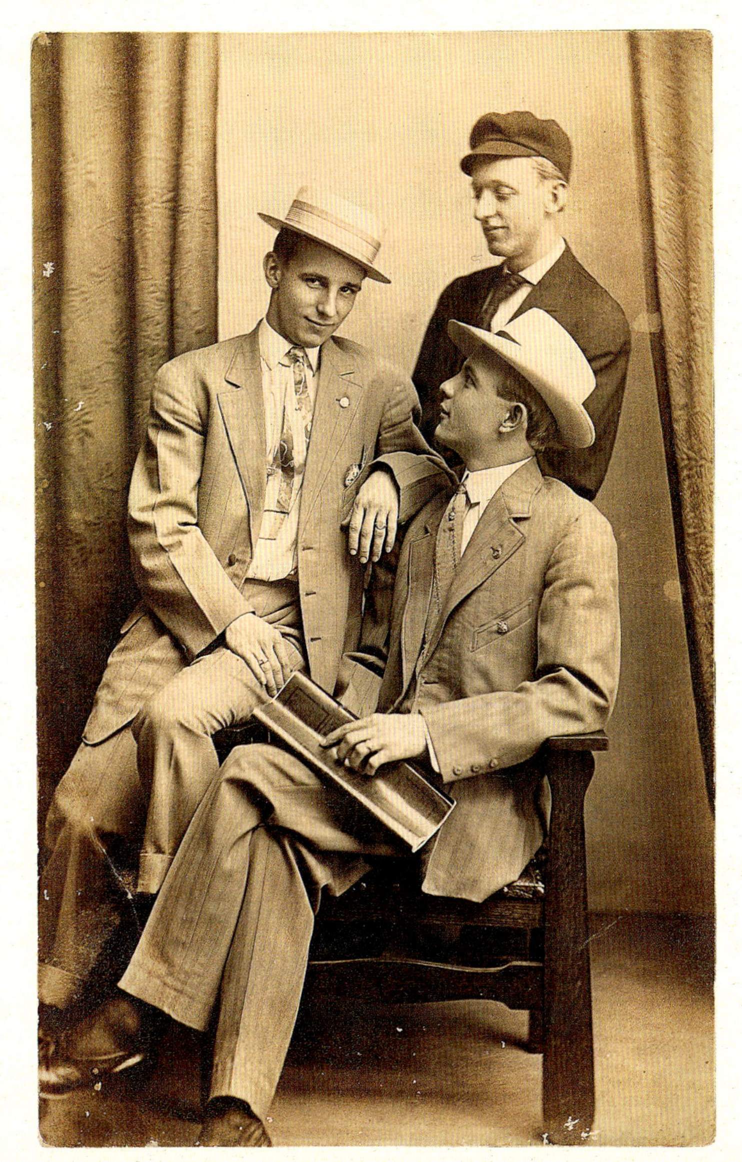

America 1910
➤ *America c. 1855*

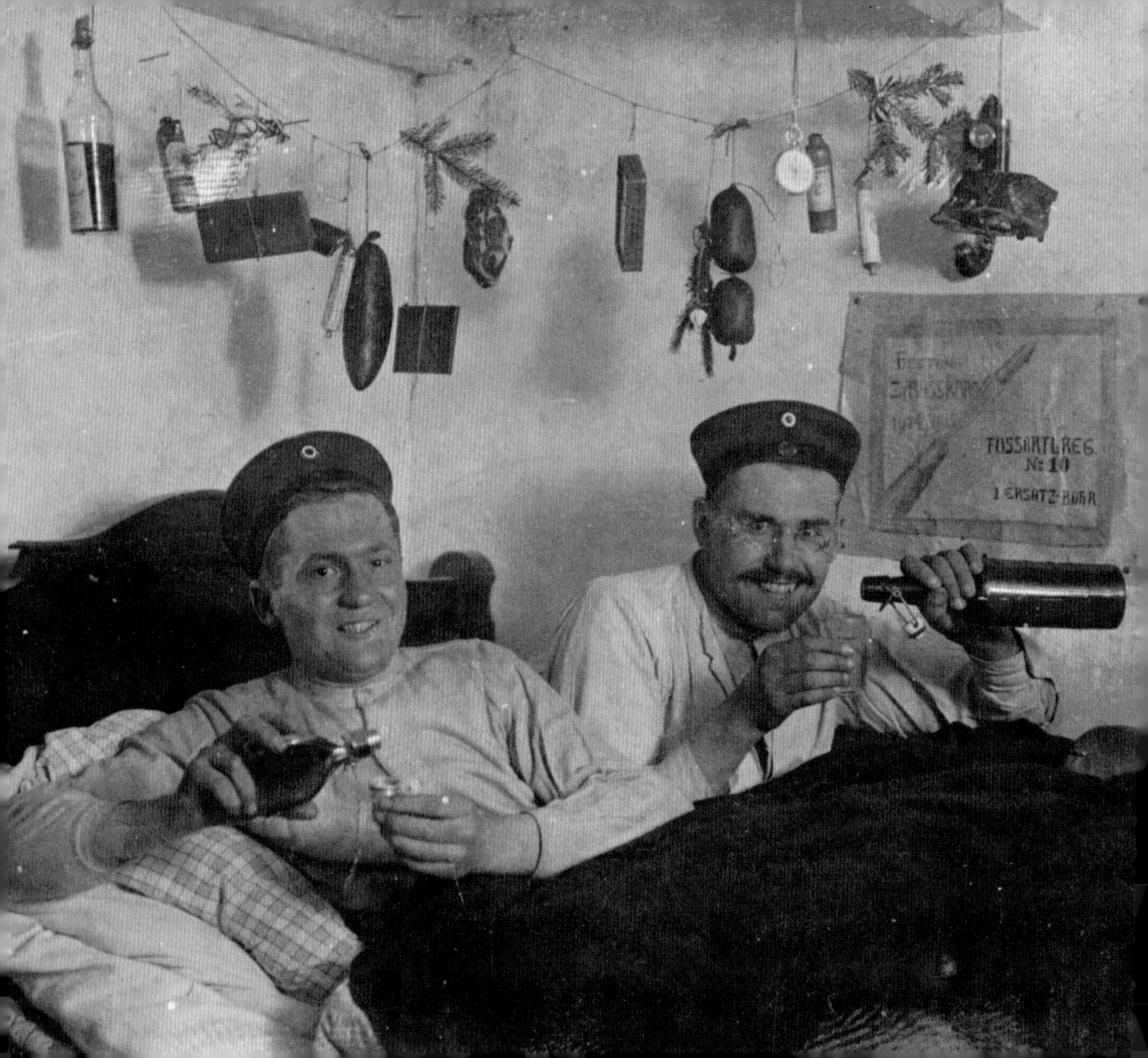
FUSSARTL.REG.
№ 10

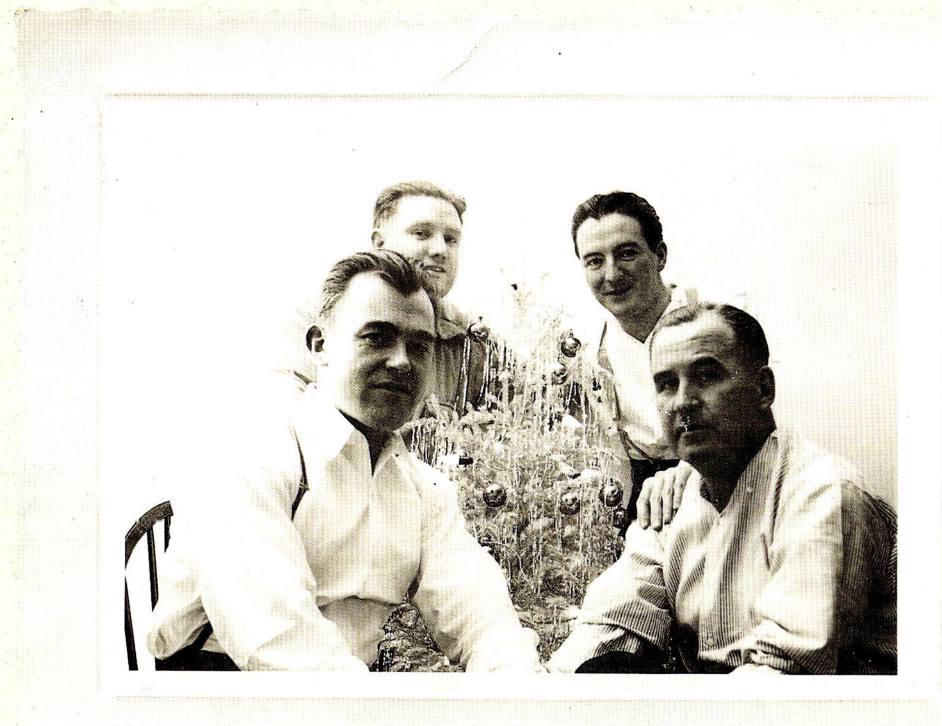

America 1940's
< Germany 1914–15

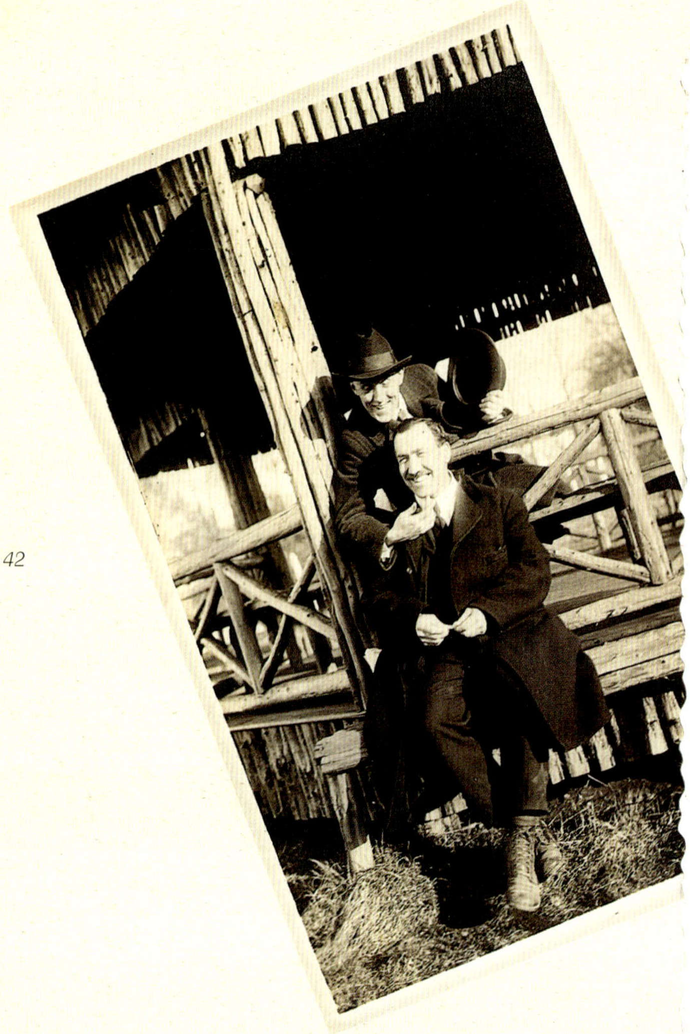

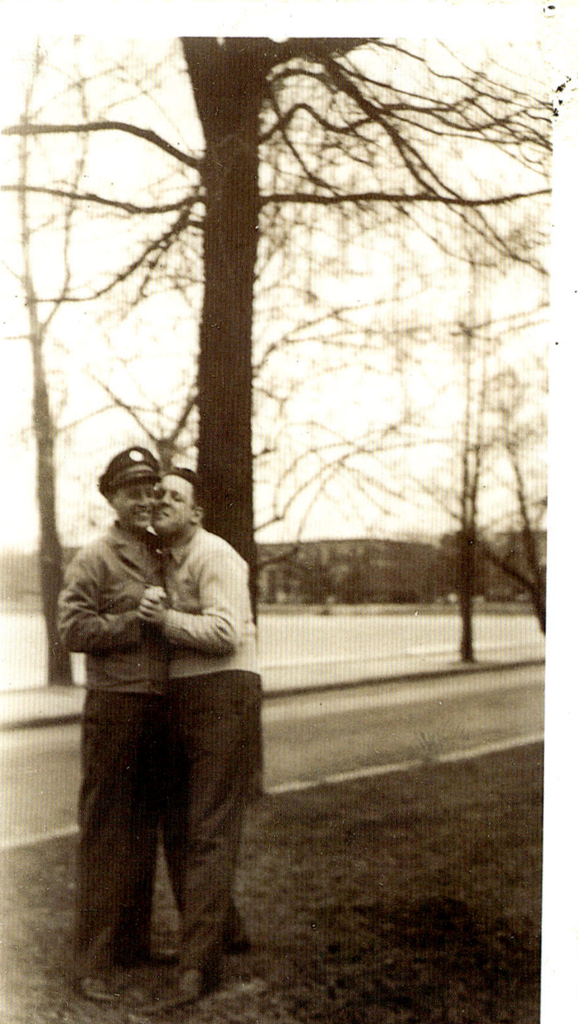

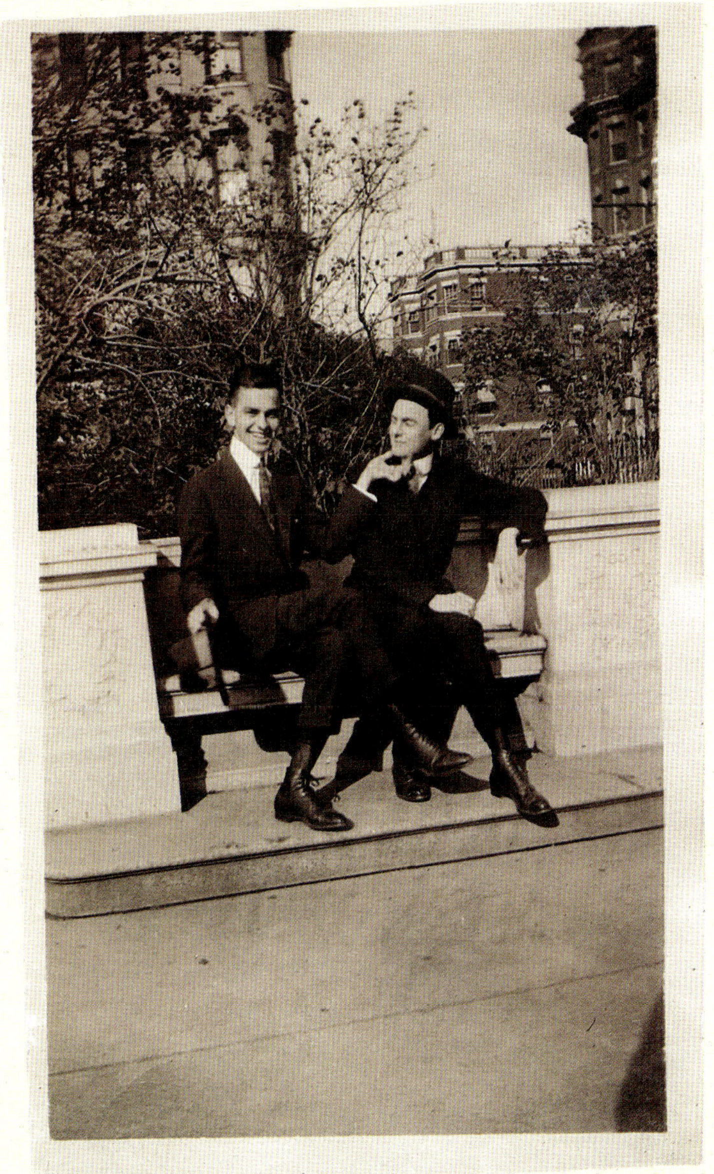

America 1910–12
≺ *America 1920's*
≺ *America early 1940's*

Say Burt!!
Who's your friend

France c. 1900
≺ America 1907–08

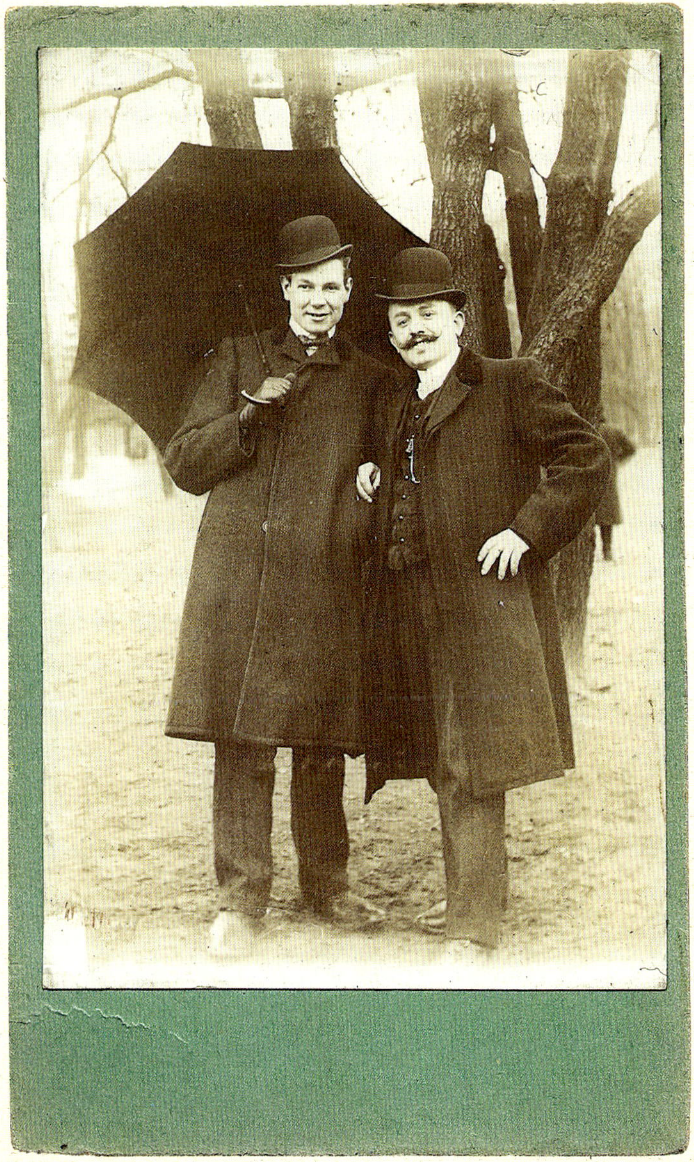

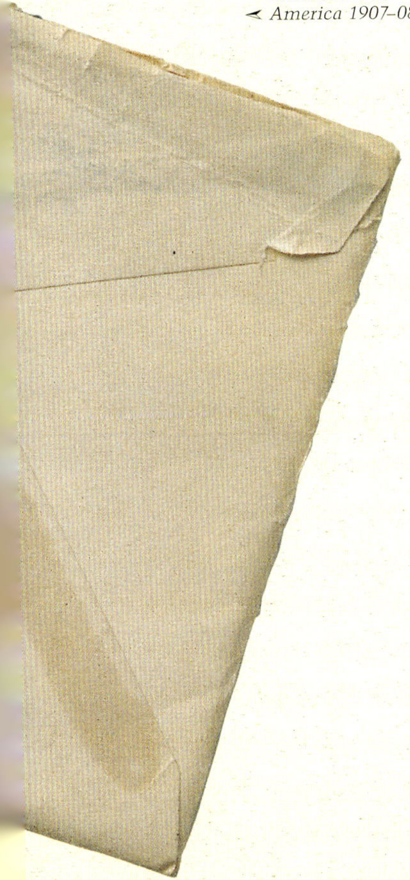

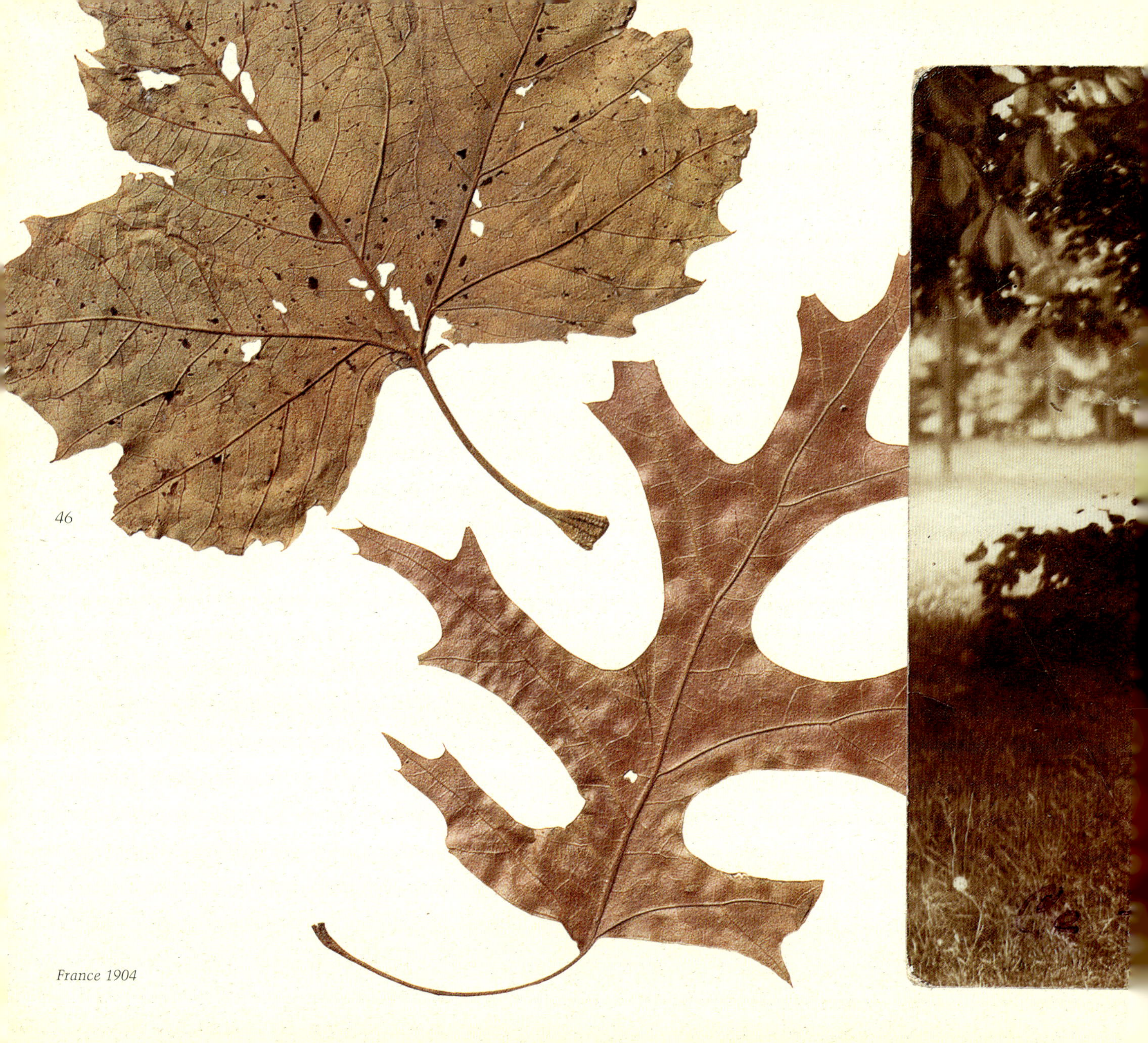

France 1904

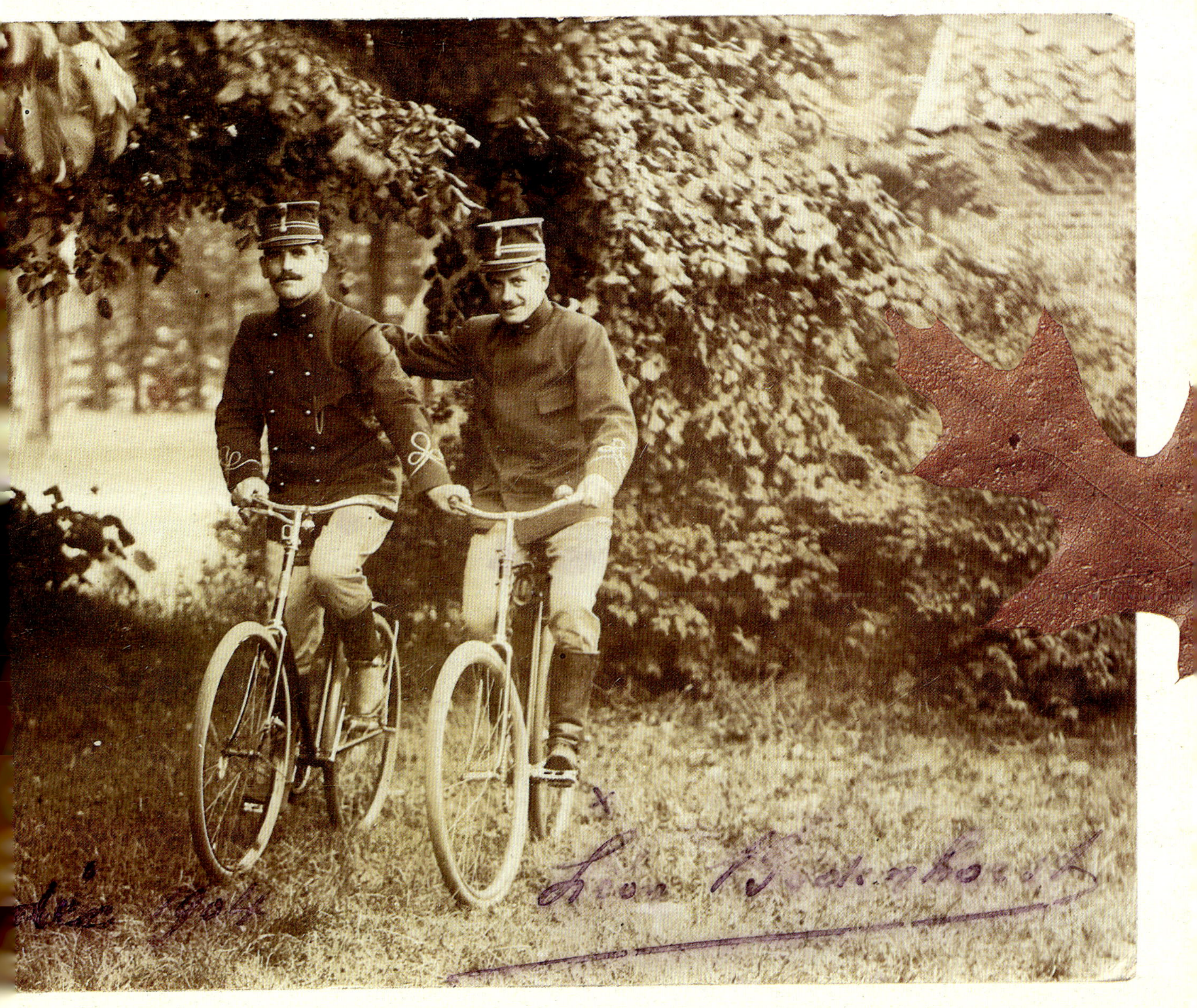

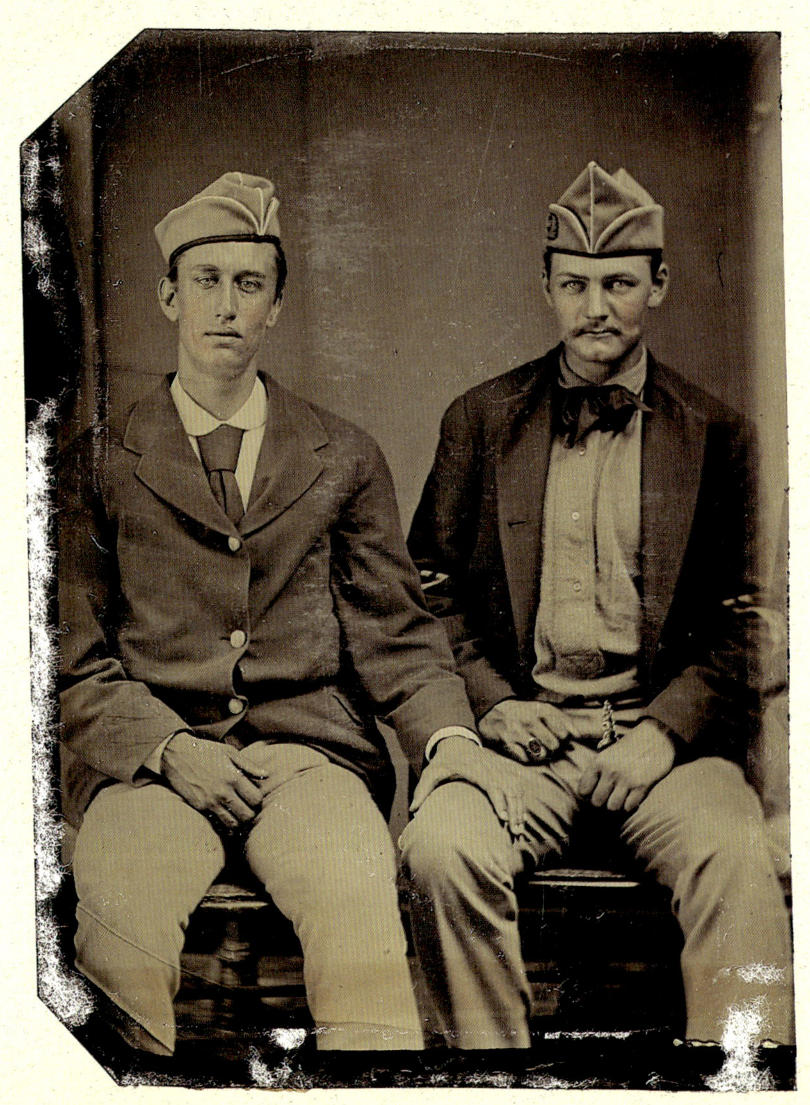

America/Canada 1870's
America/Canada 1870's ➢

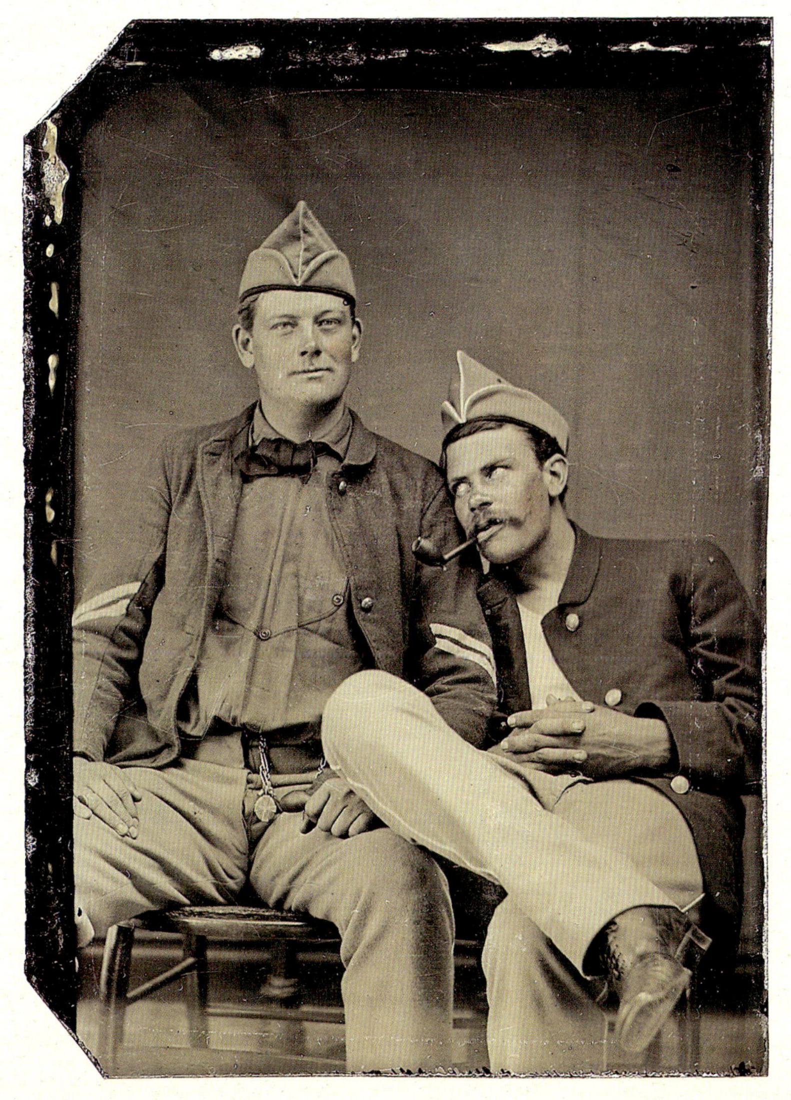

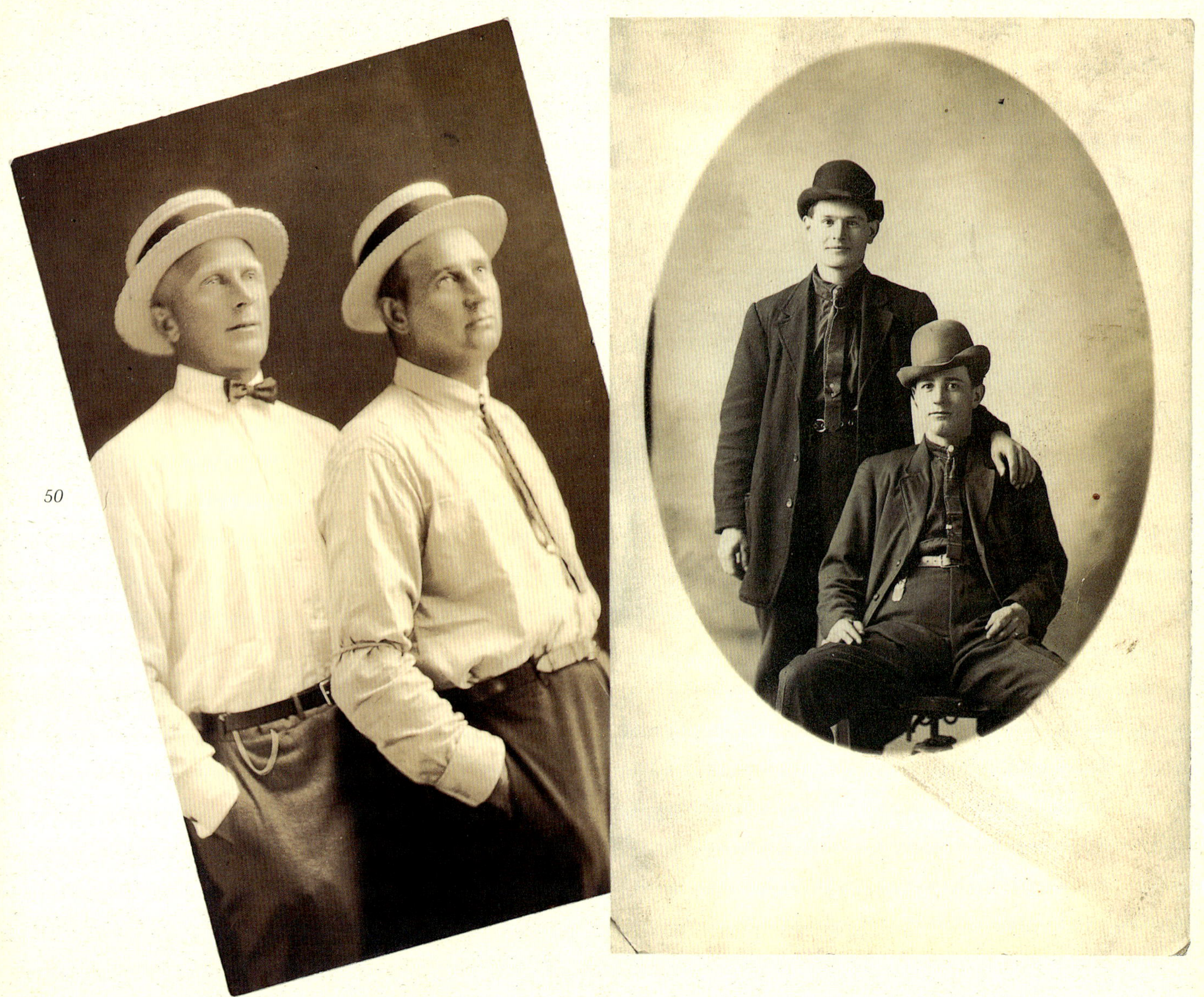

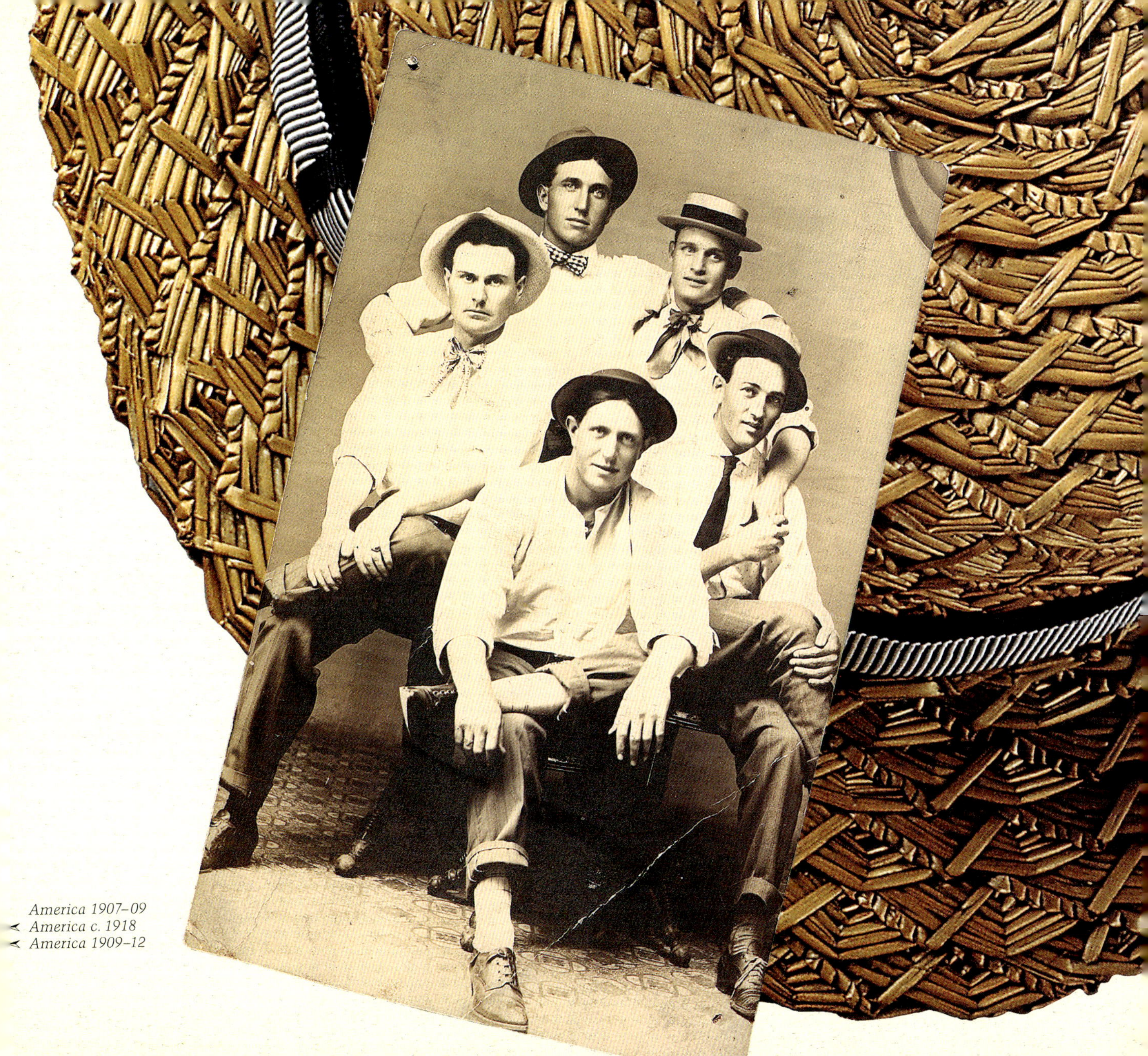

America 1907–09
< America c. 1918
< America 1909–12

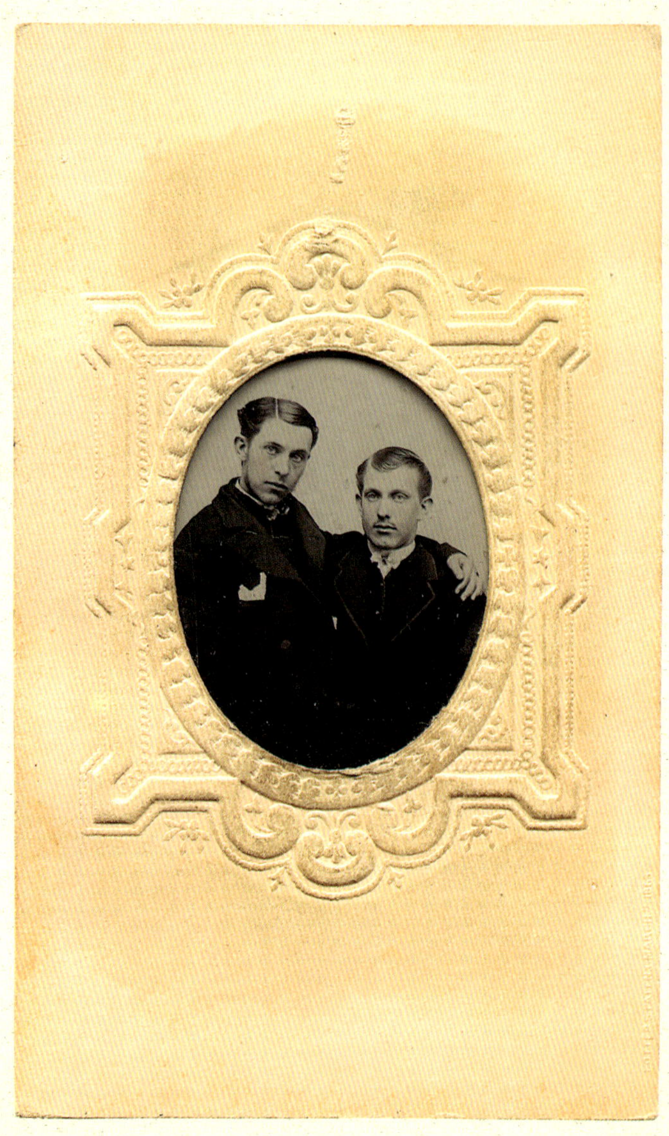

America c. 1865
America c. 1875 ➢

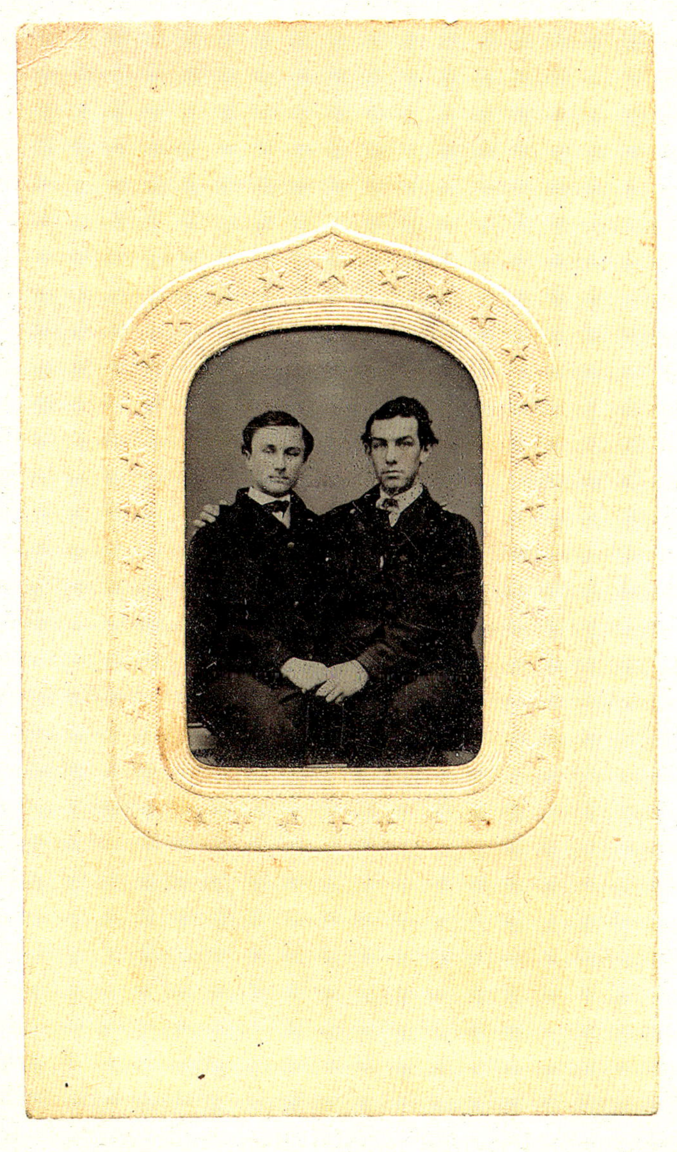

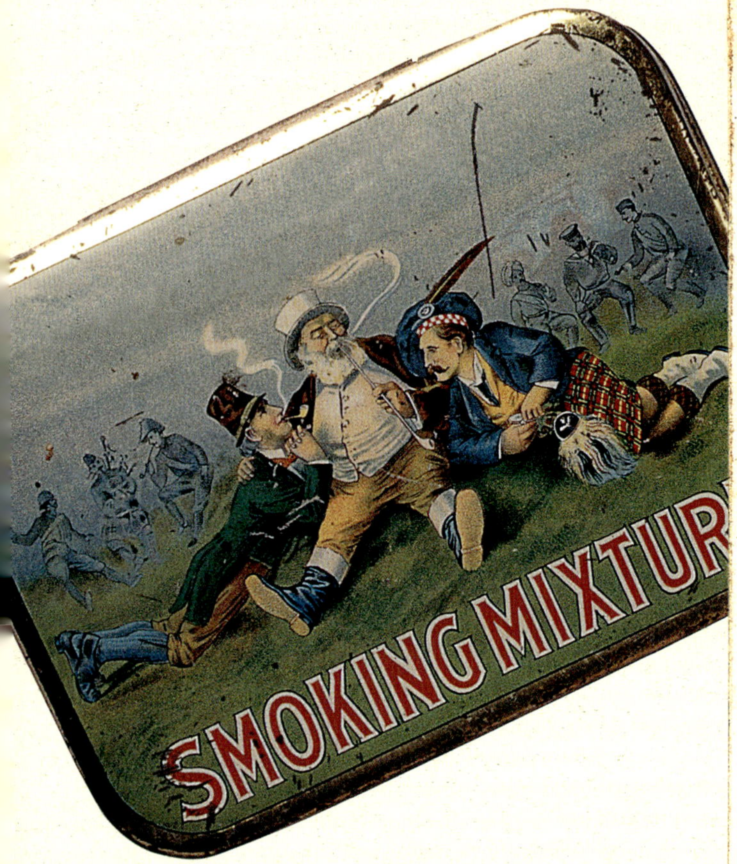

Scotland early 1880's
America 1915 ➢

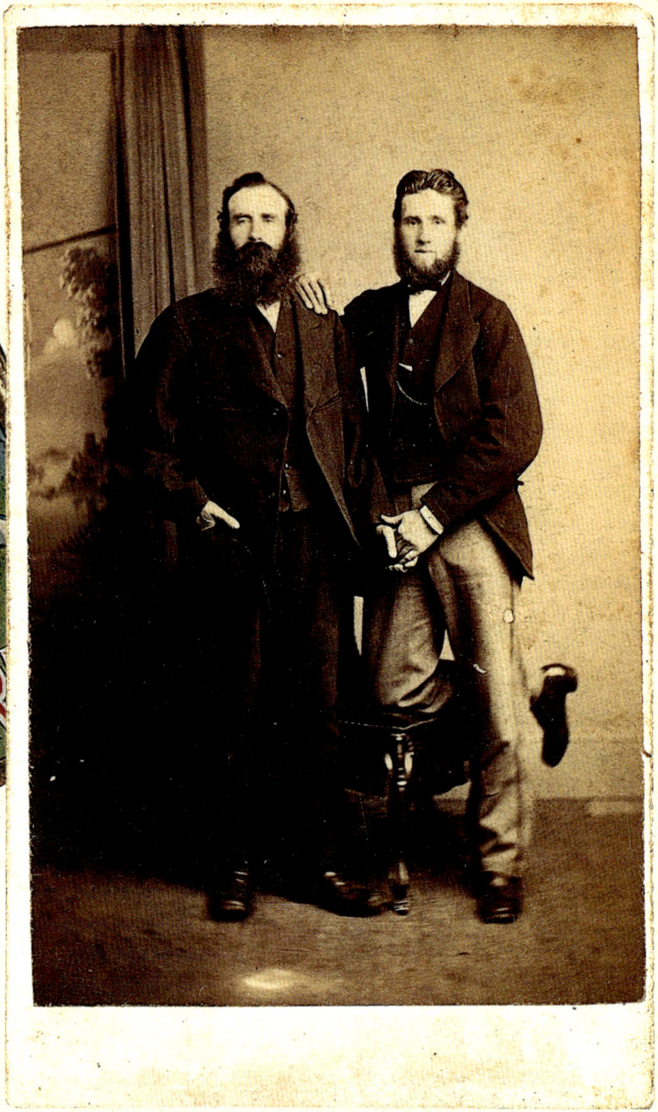

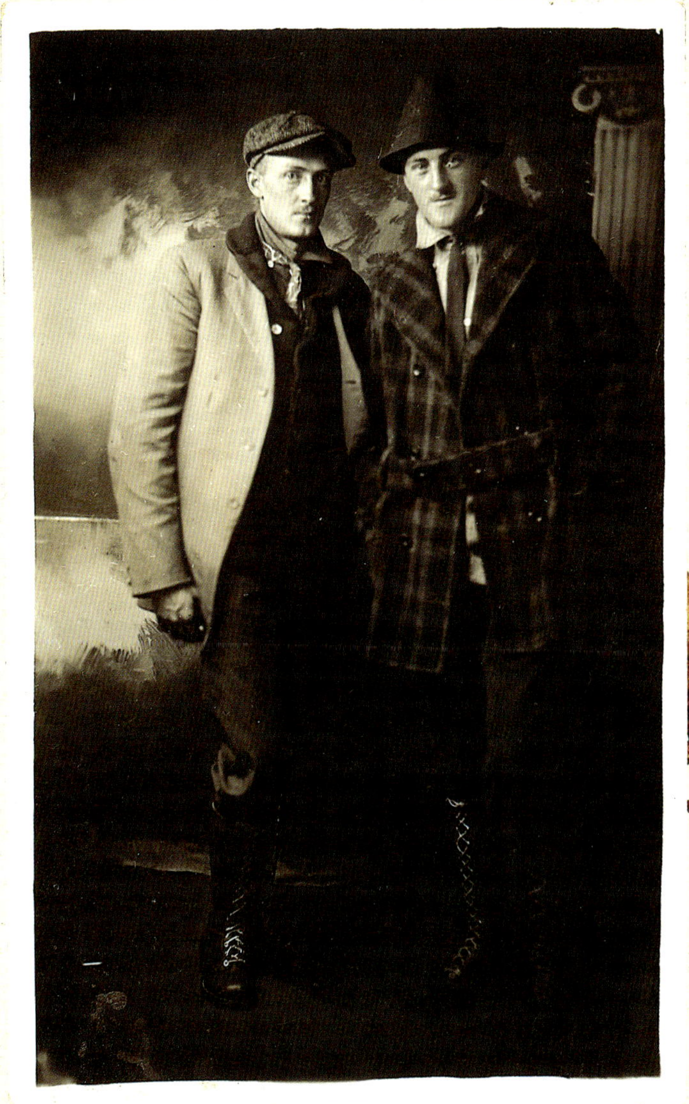

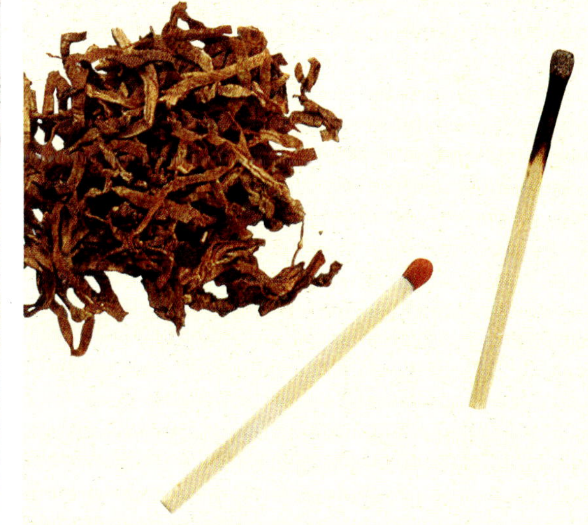

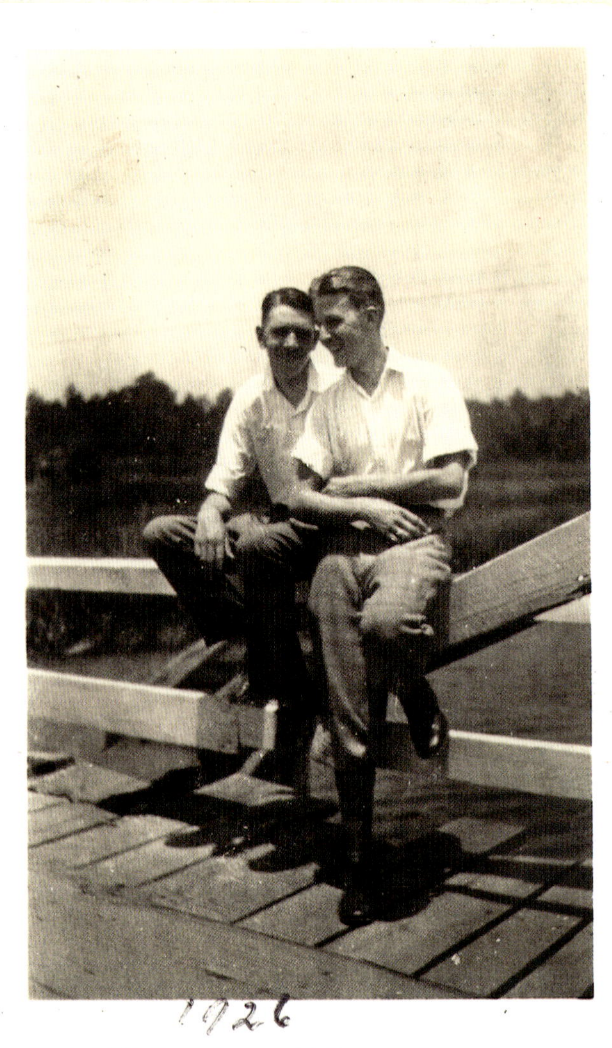

America 1926
America 1935 ➢

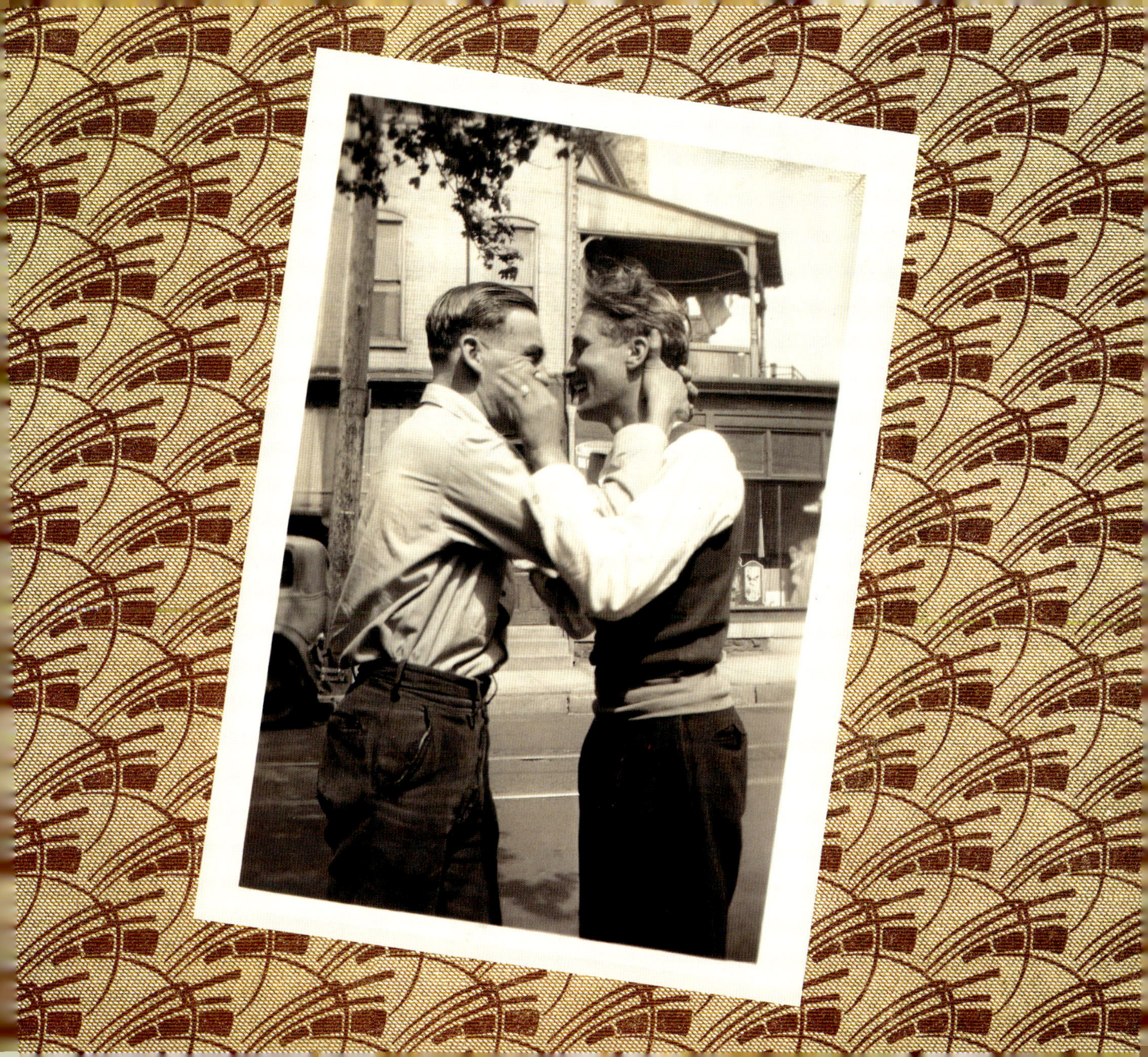

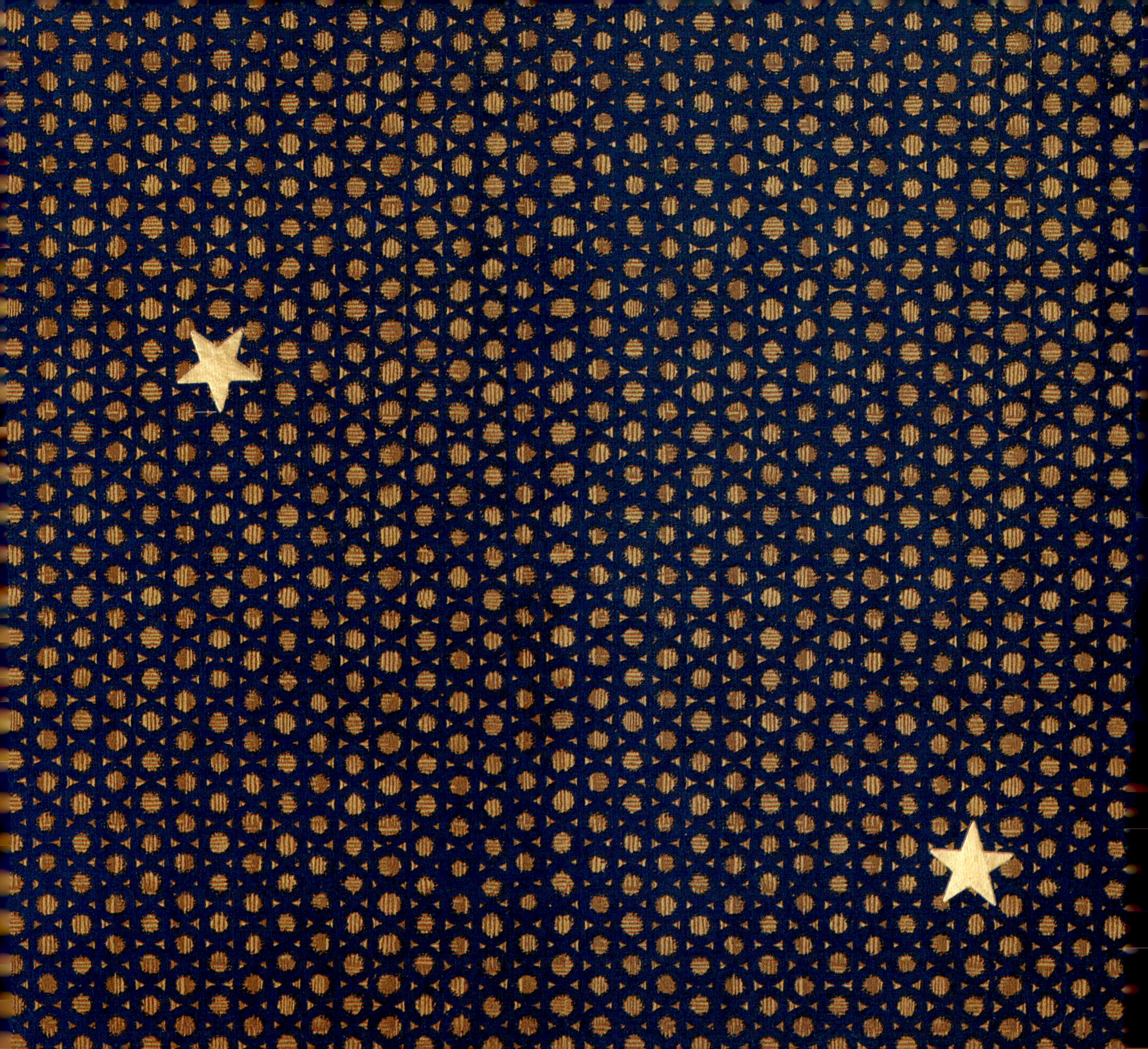

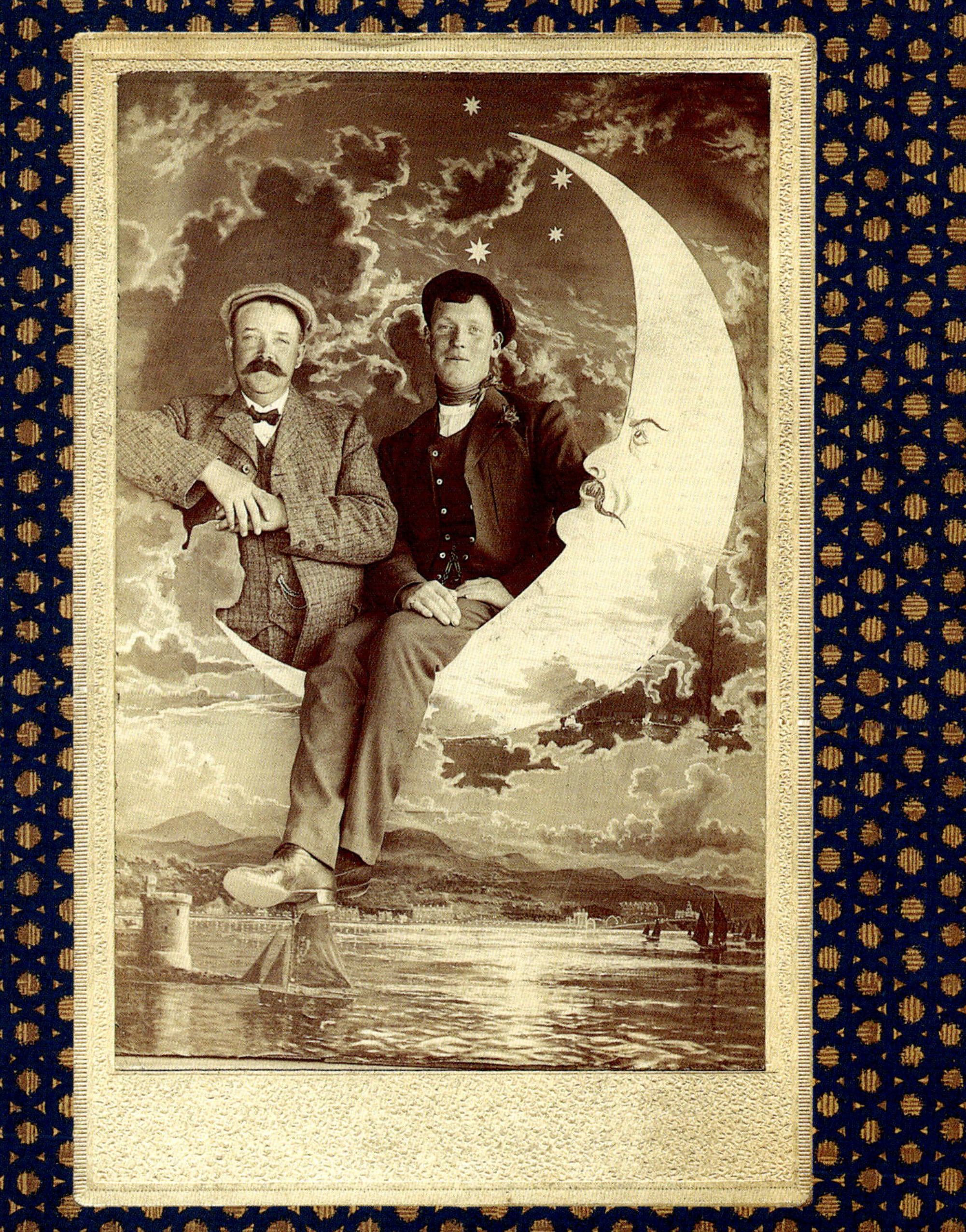

England c. 1890

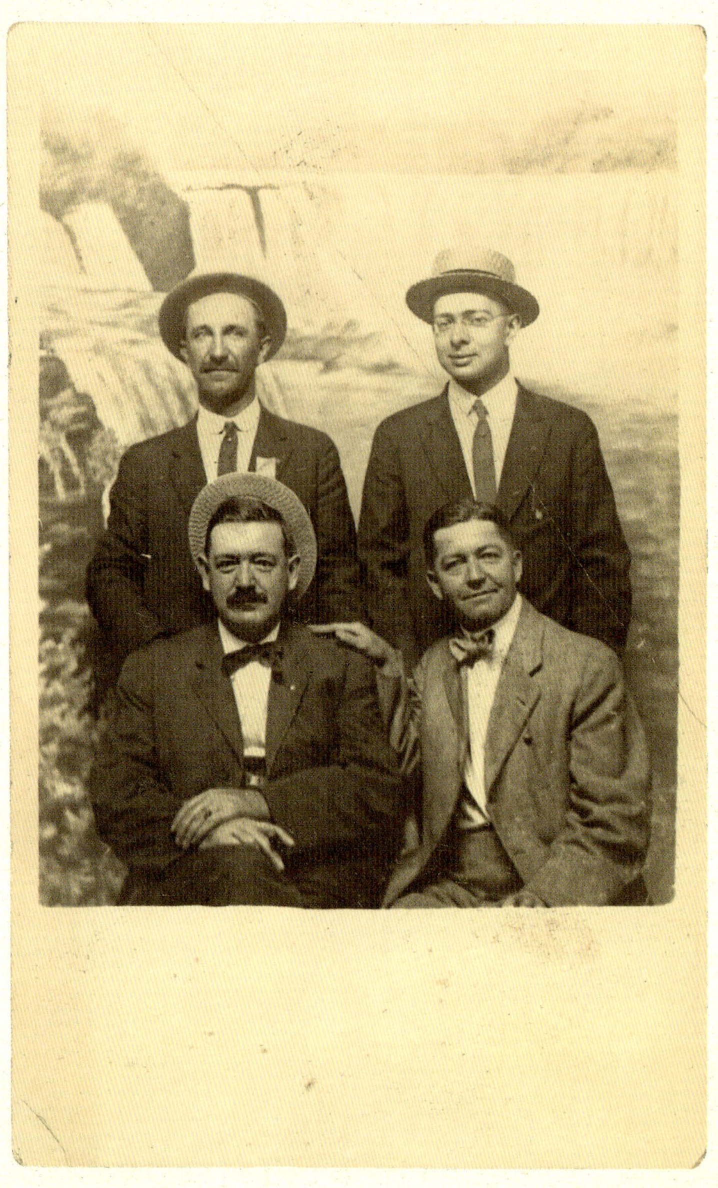

America c. 1910
Japan late 1940's ➢

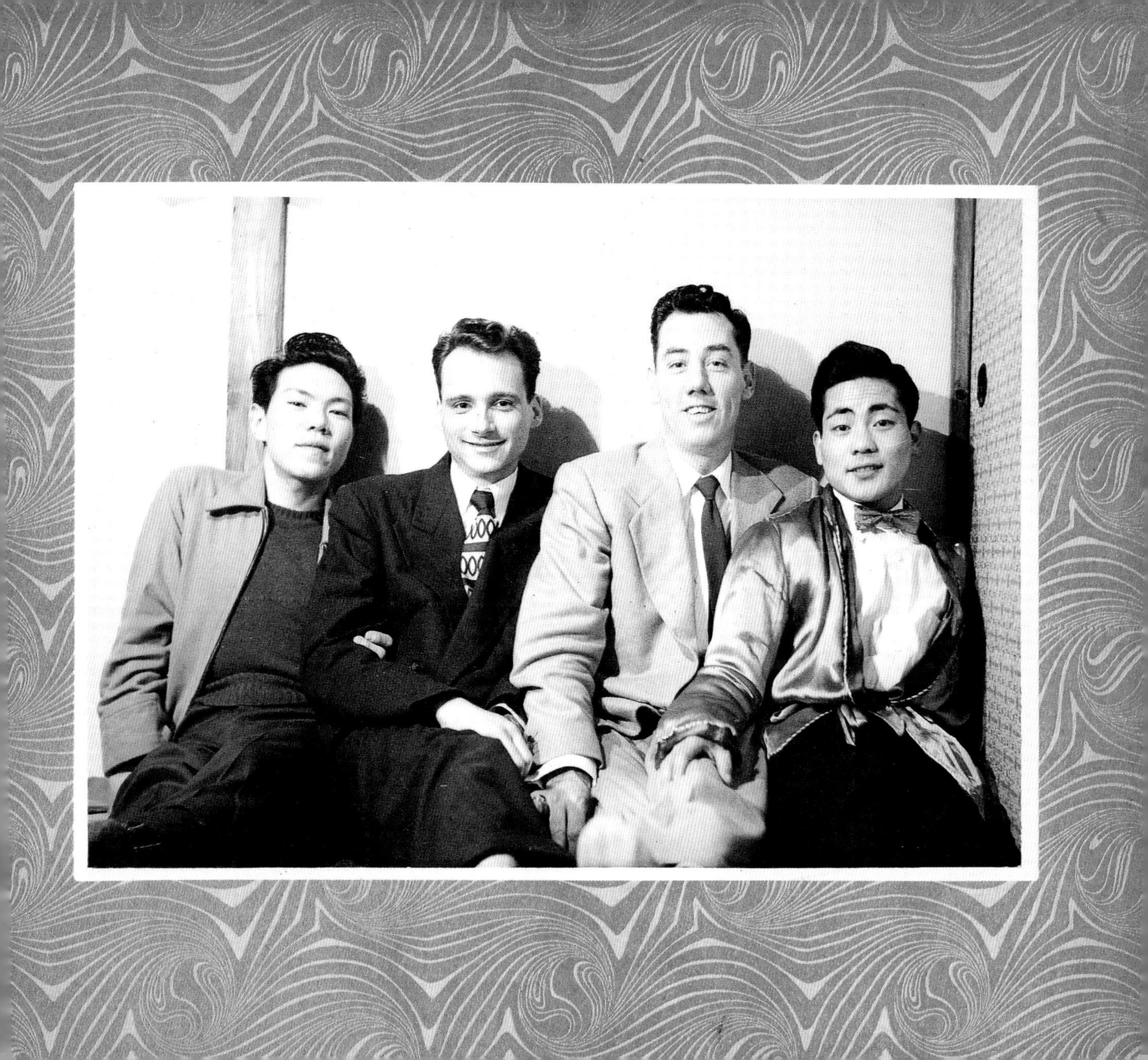

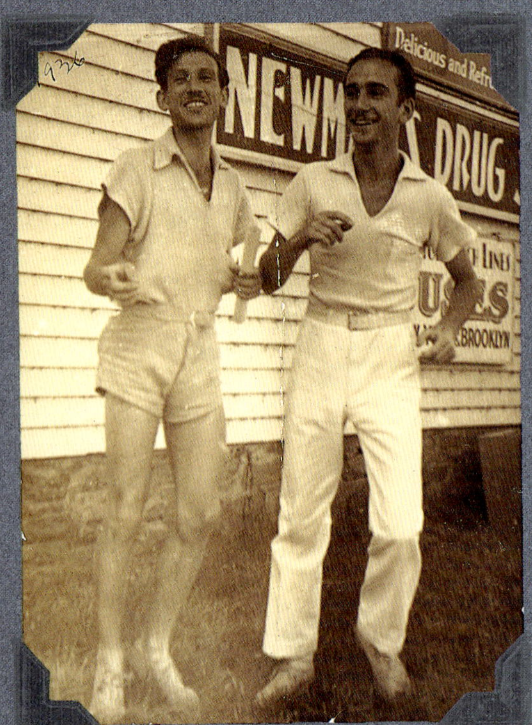

America 1936

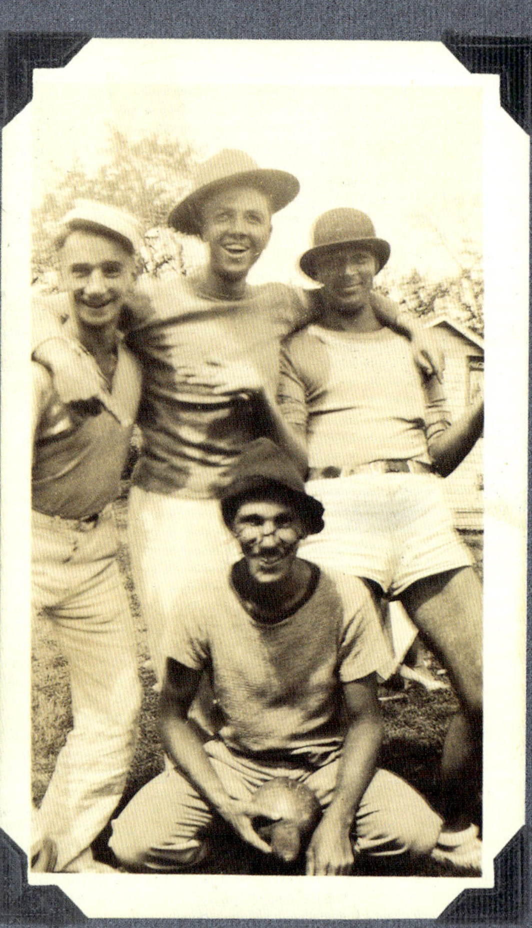

America c. 1930

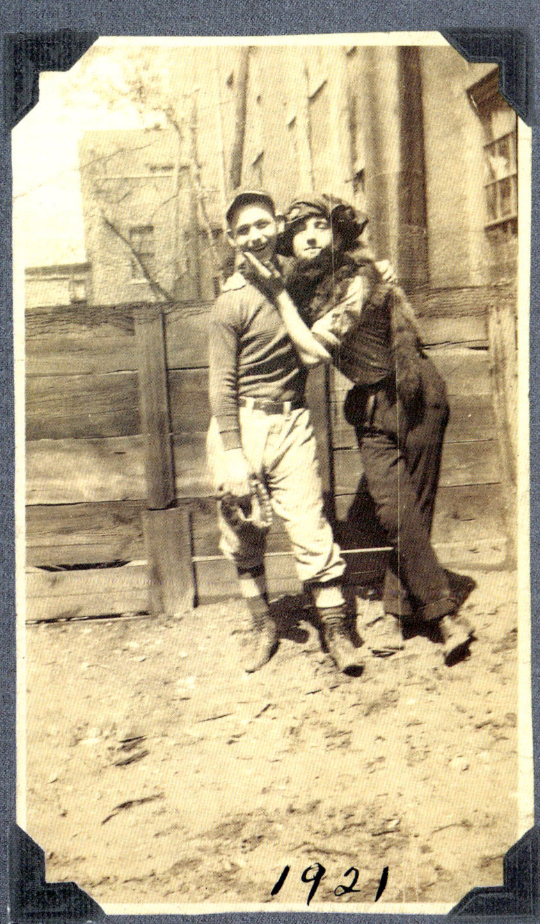

America 1921

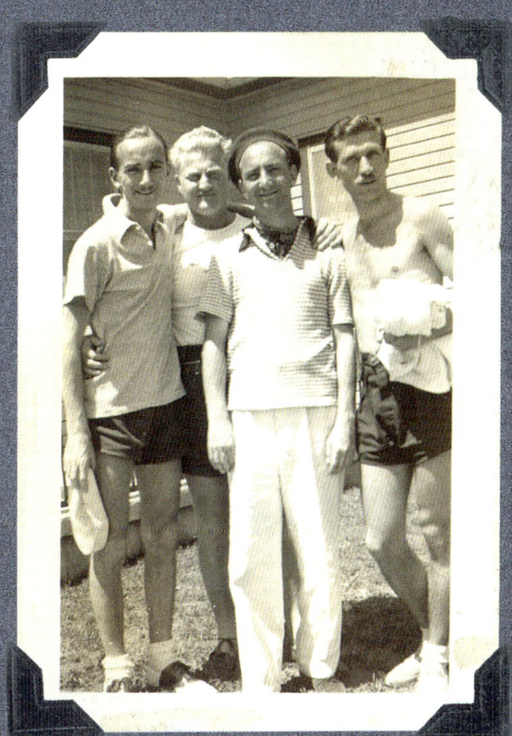
America 1938

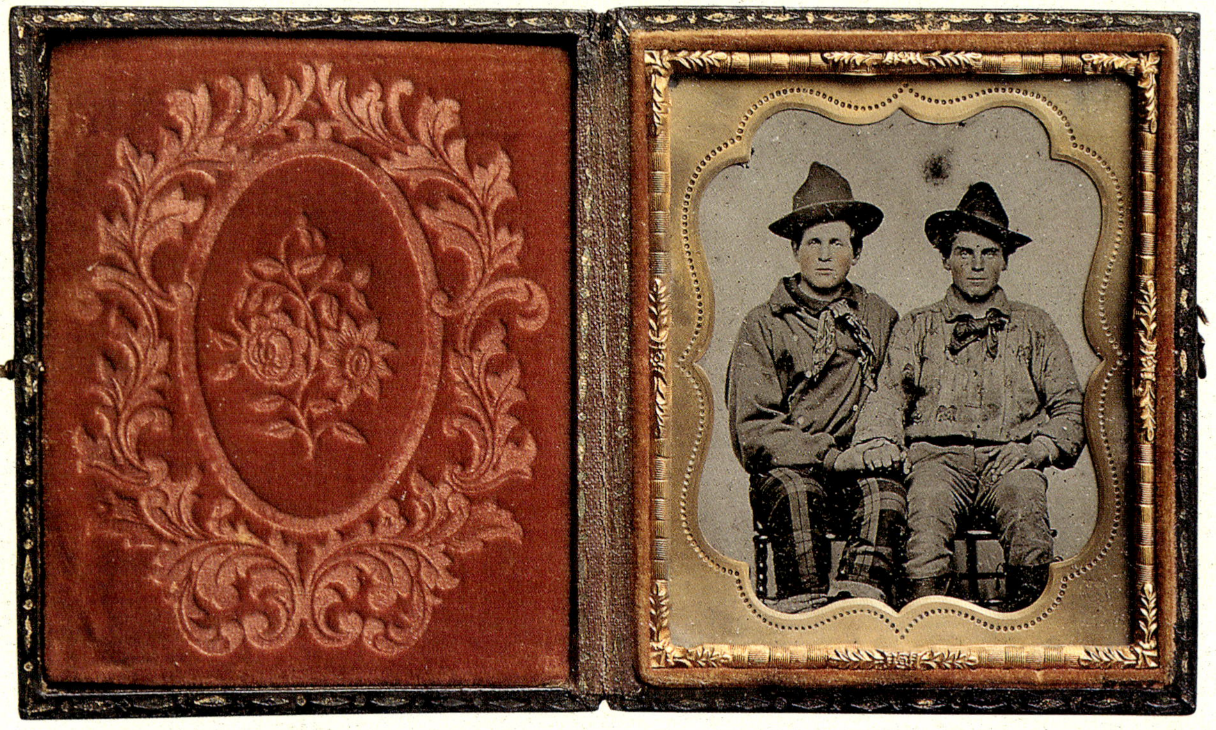

America c. 1855
America c. 1920 ➢

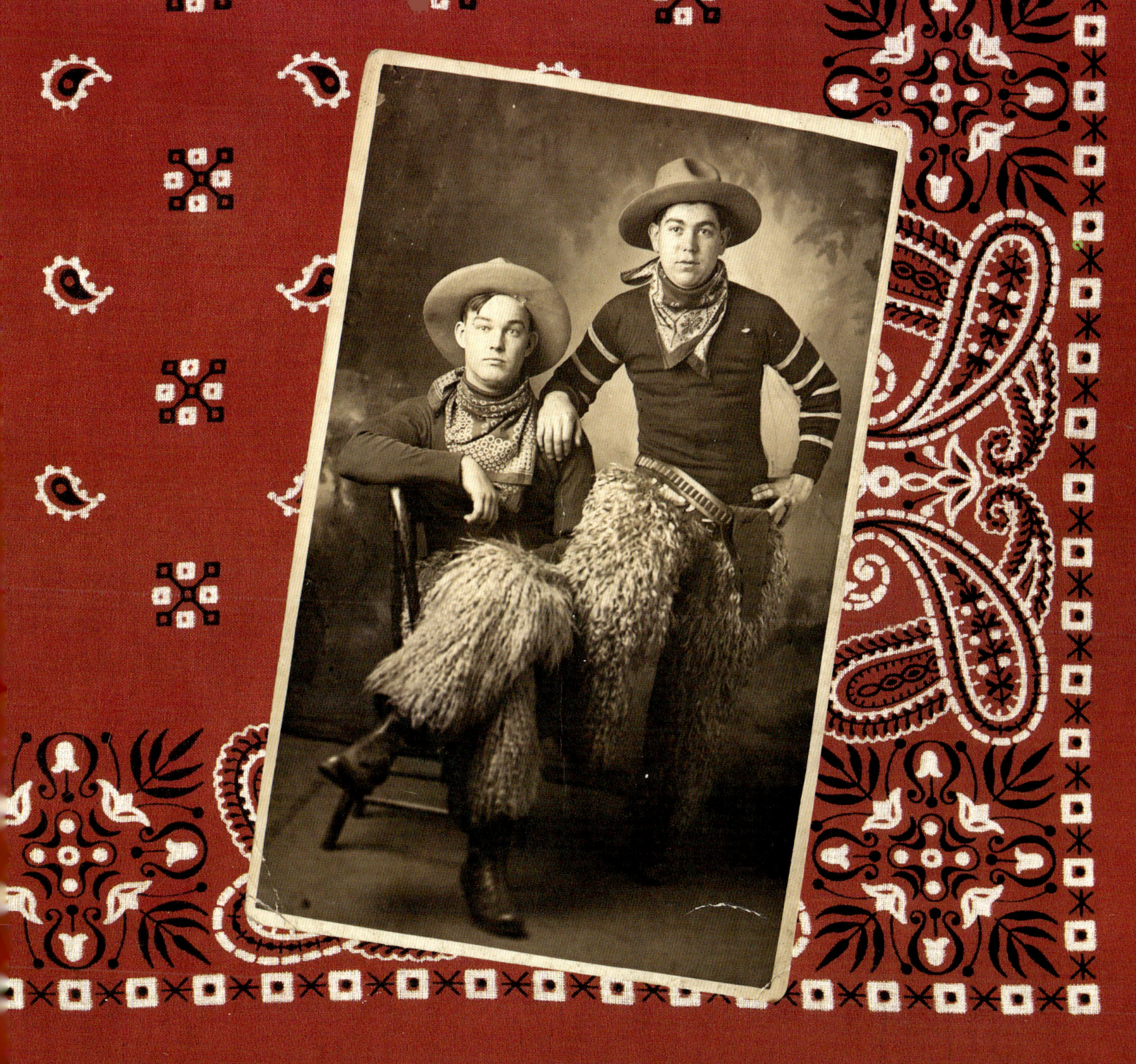

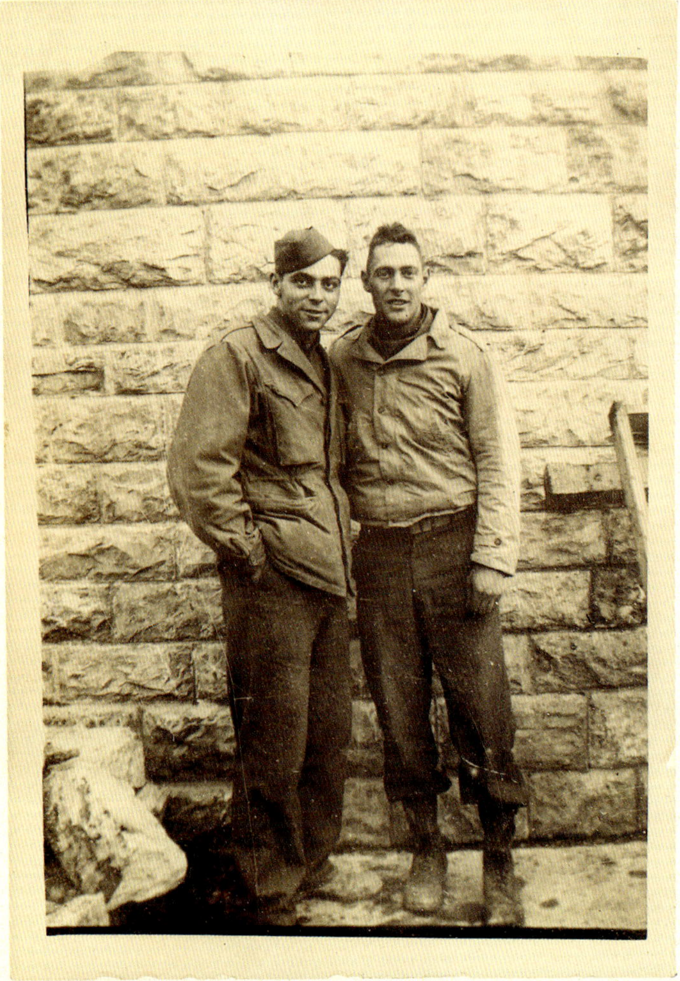

America early 1940's

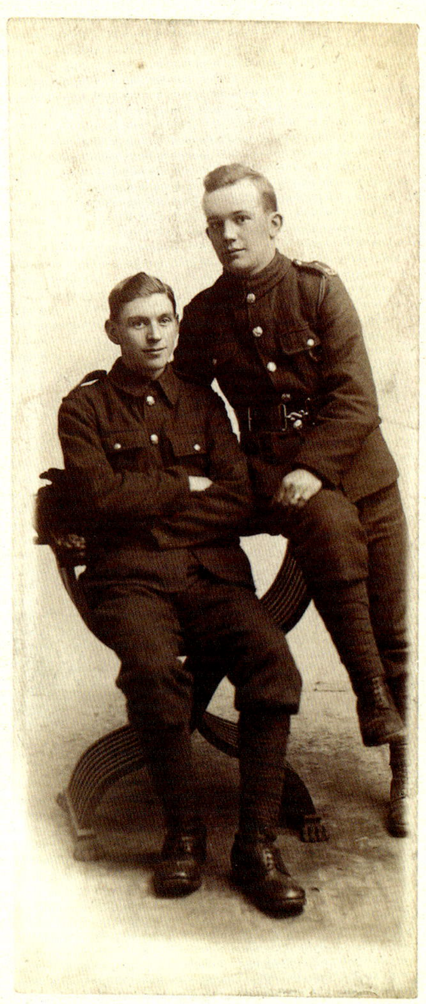

England 1900–05

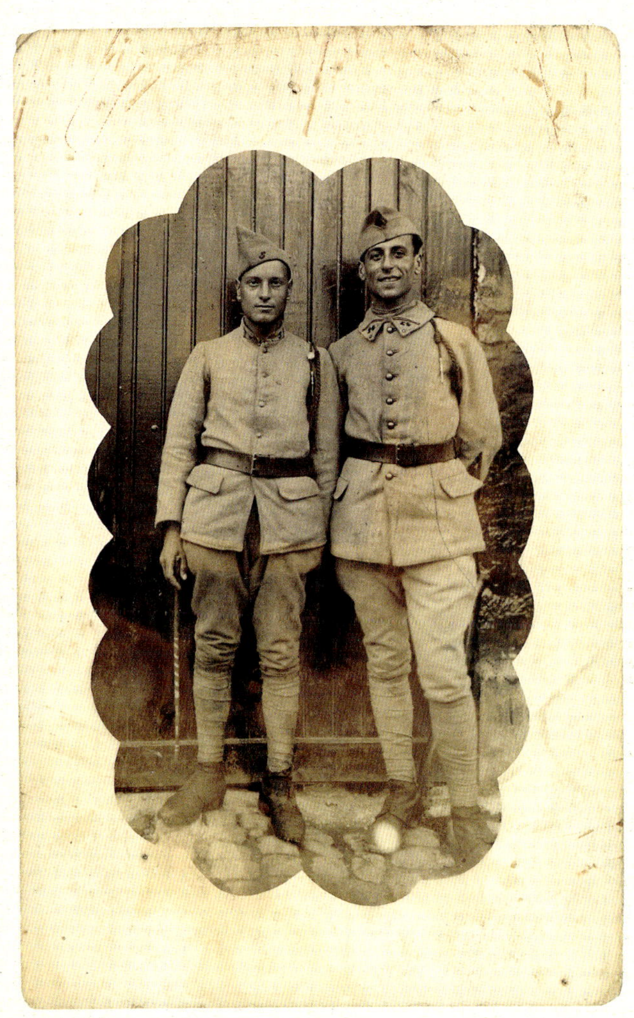

France 1915–18

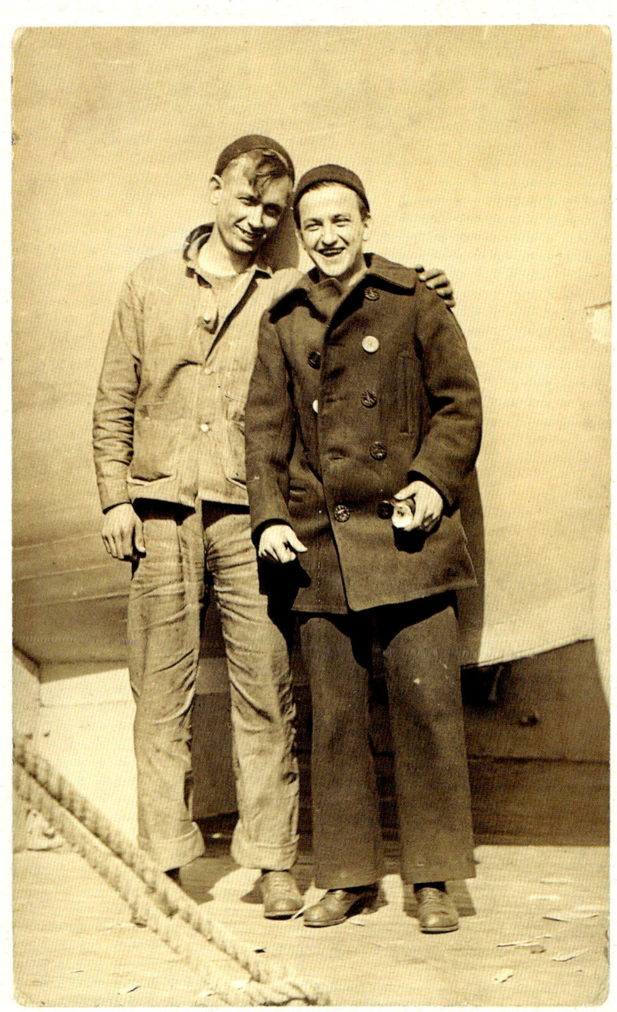

America 1918–22

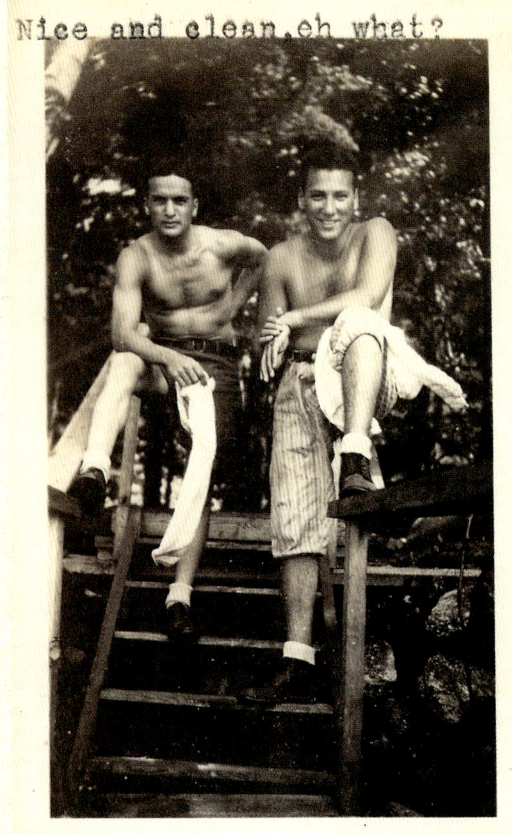

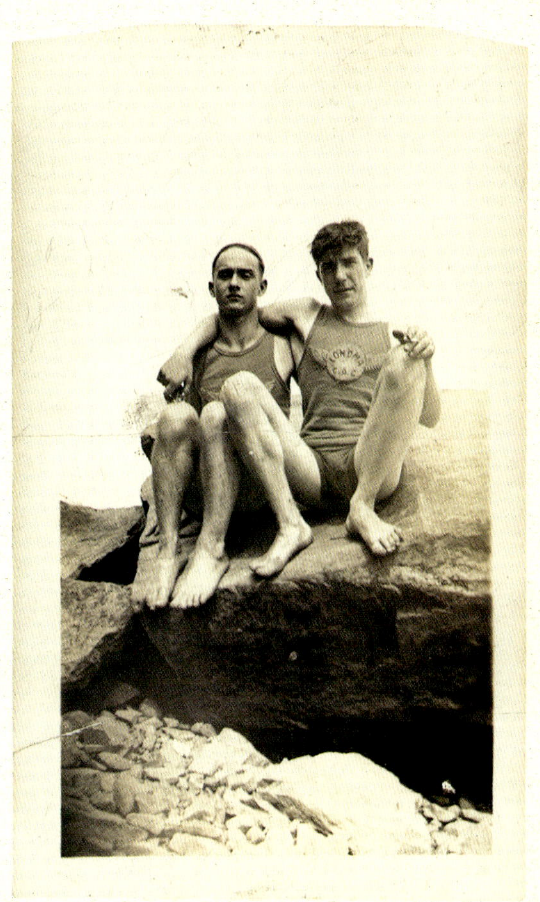

America c. 1930
America mid-1920's
America 1929–30 ➢

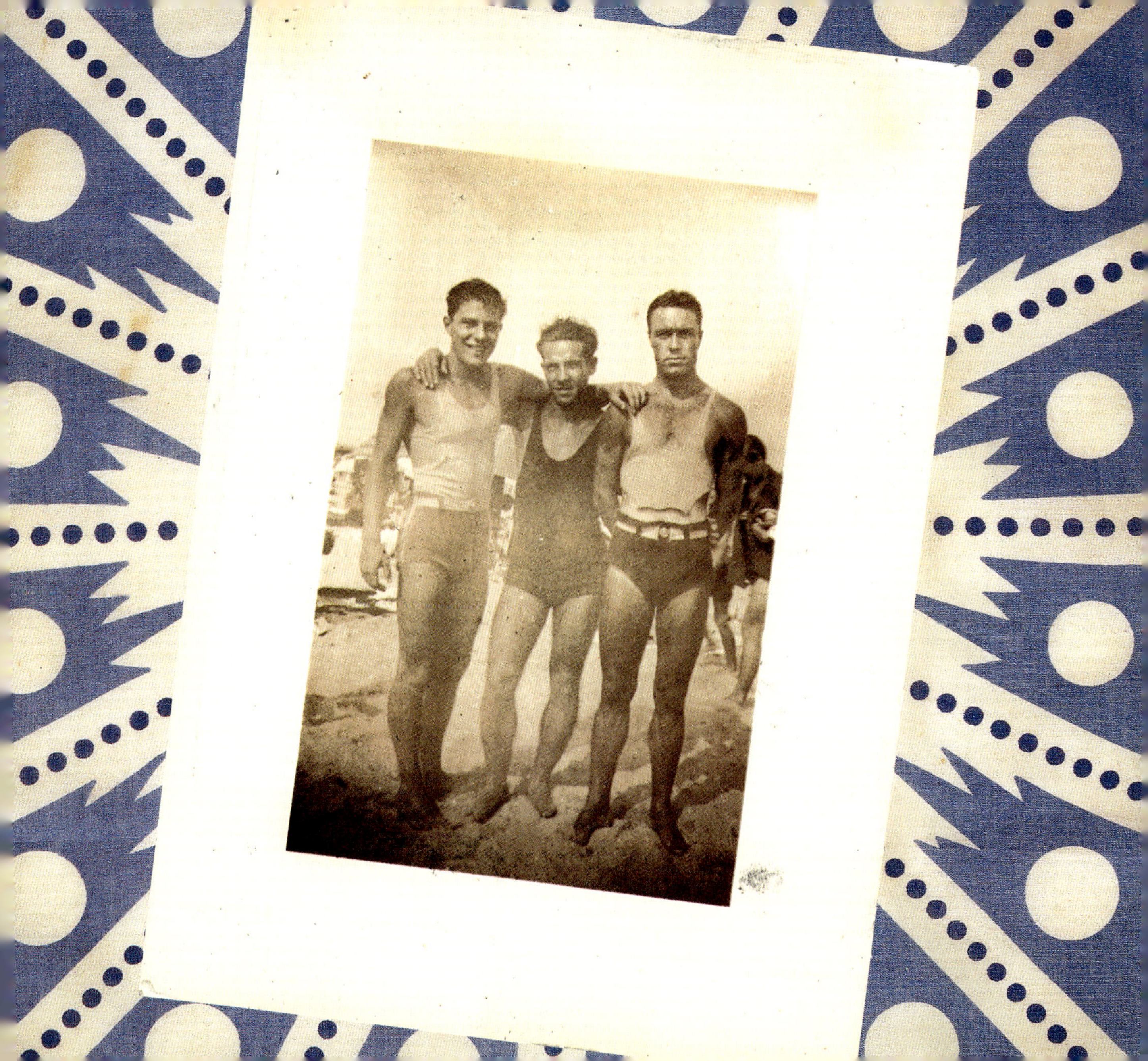

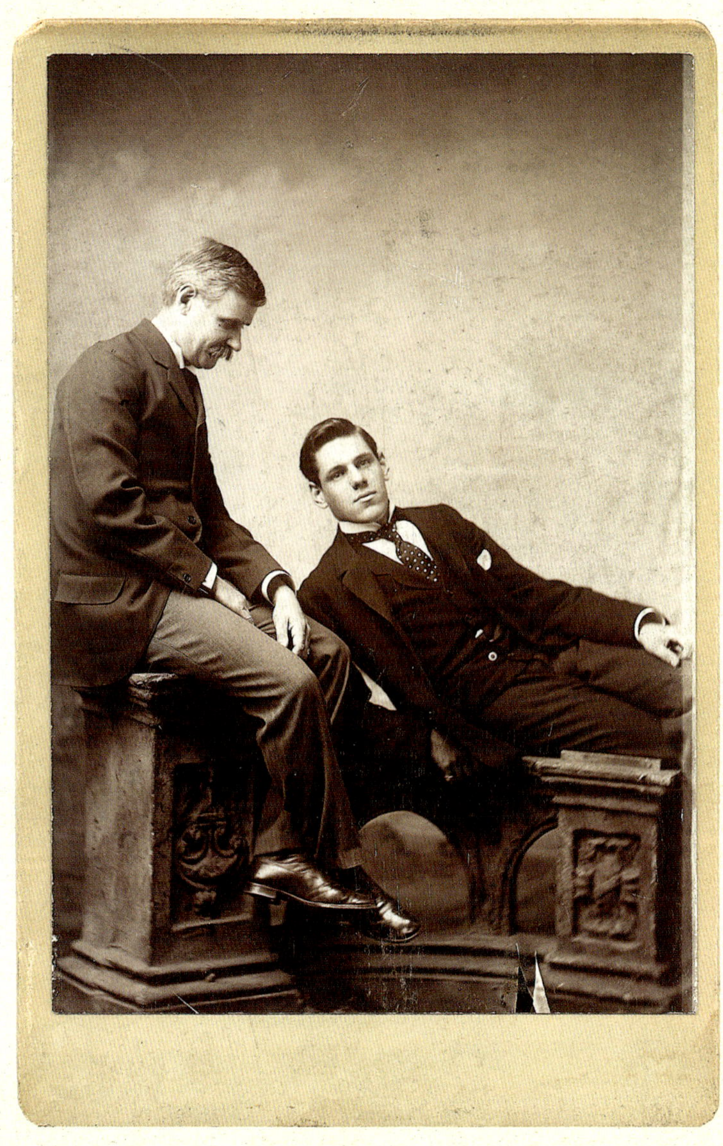

America 1895
America c. 1910 ➢

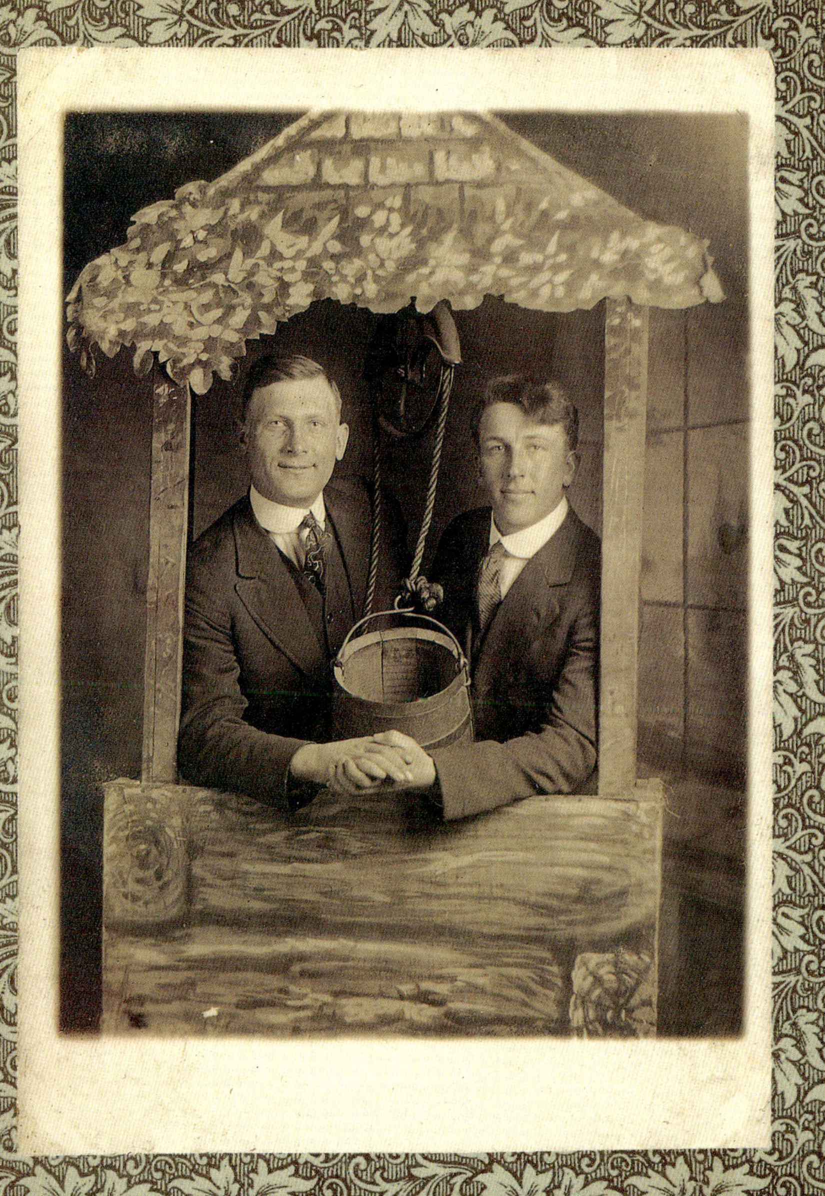

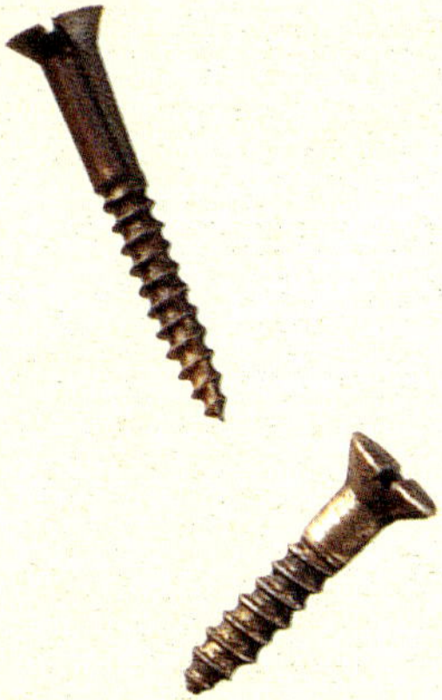

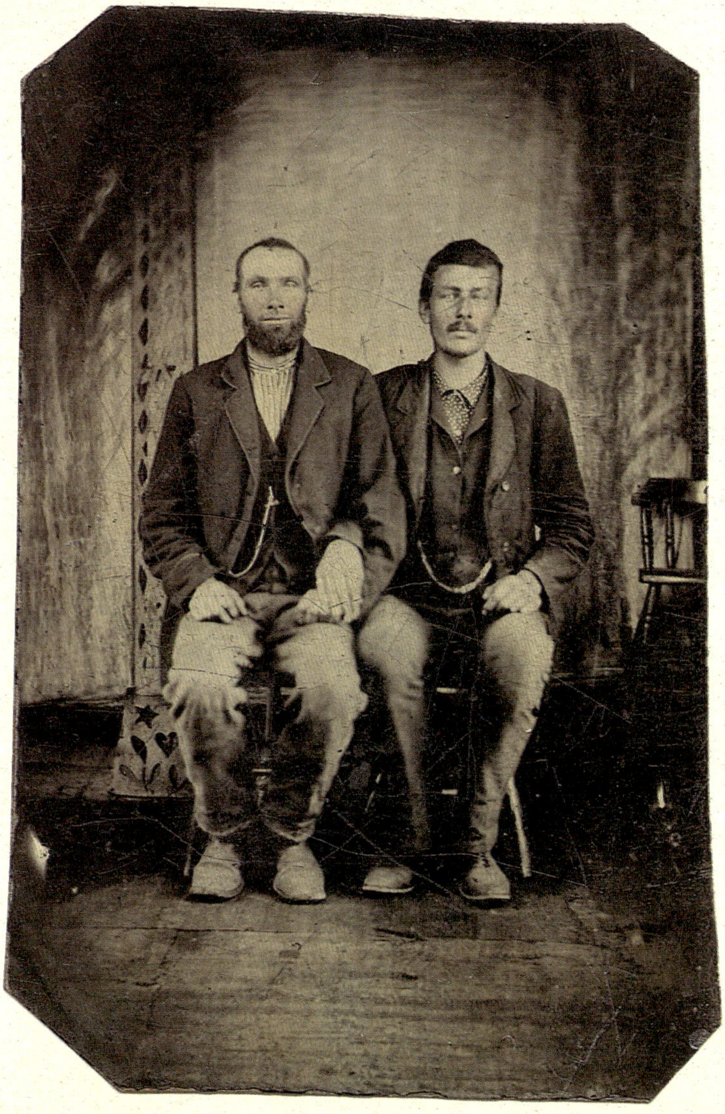

72

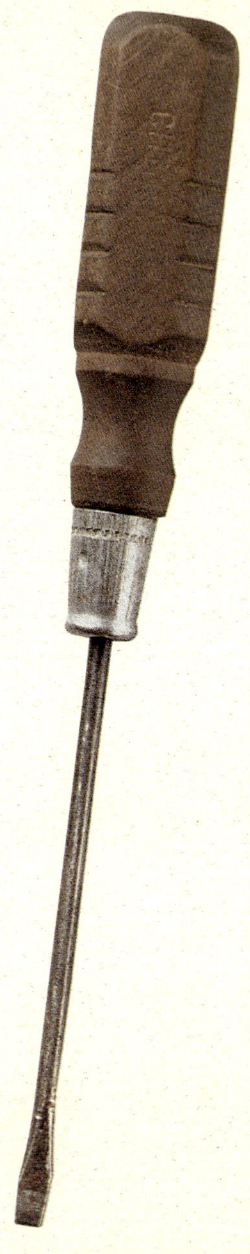

America 1865–69

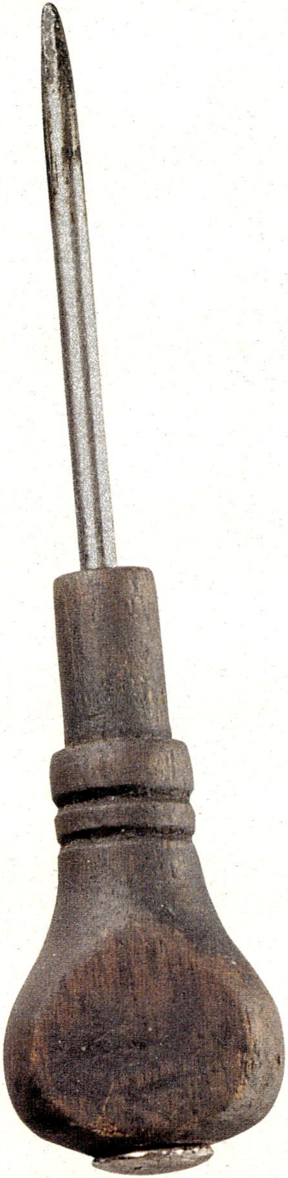

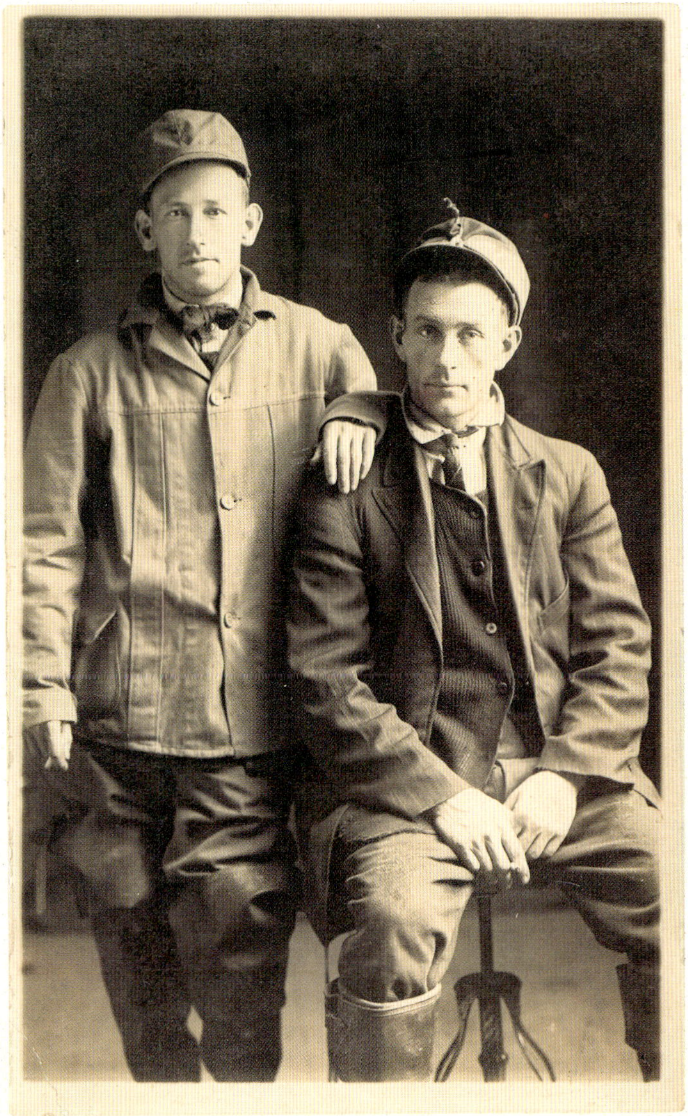

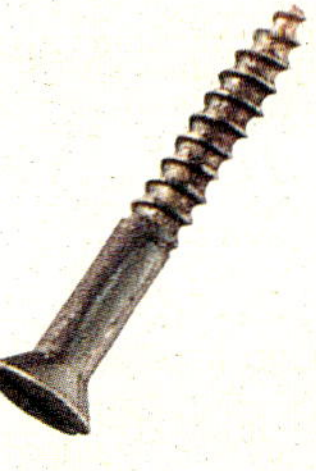

America c. 1910

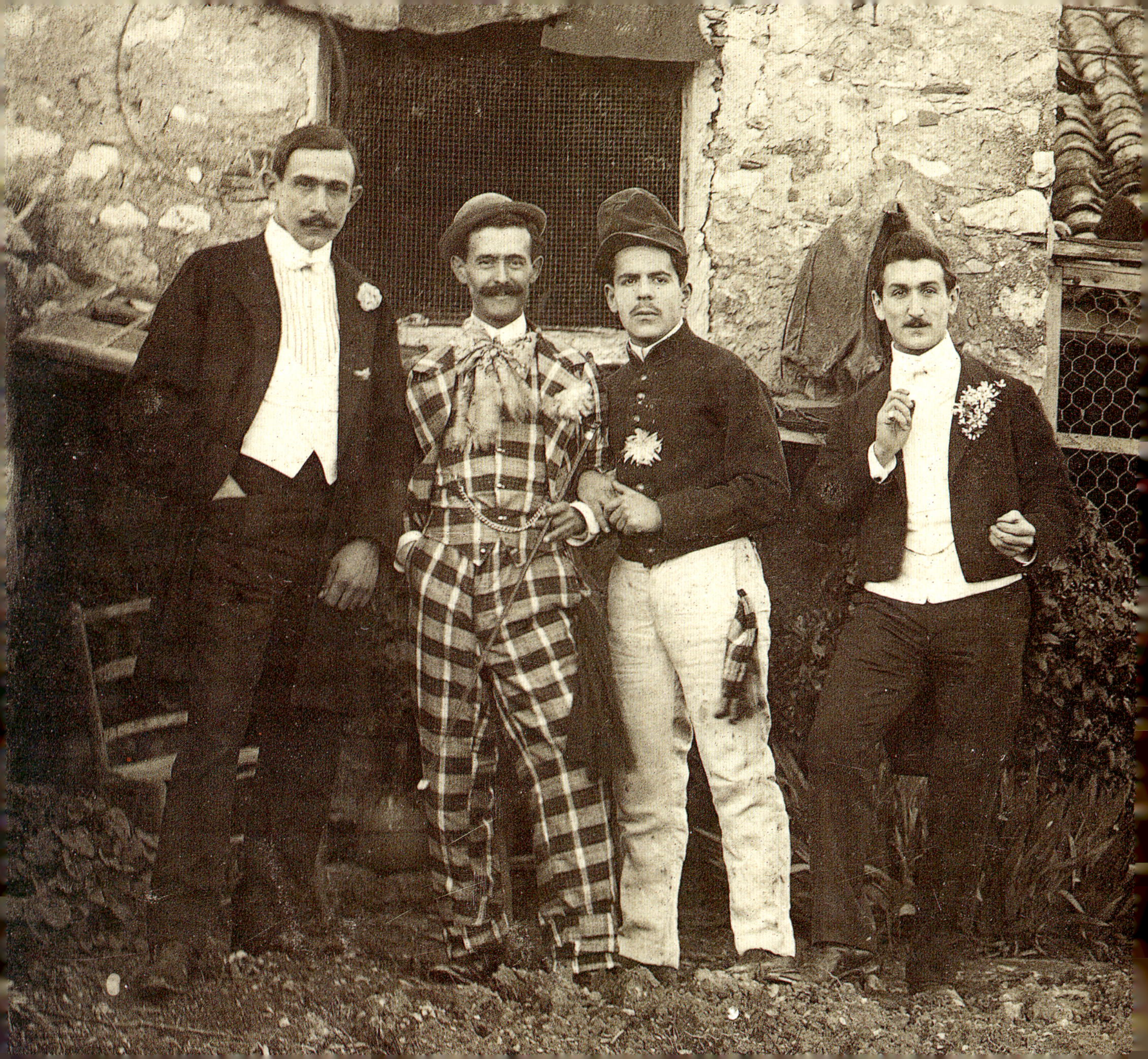

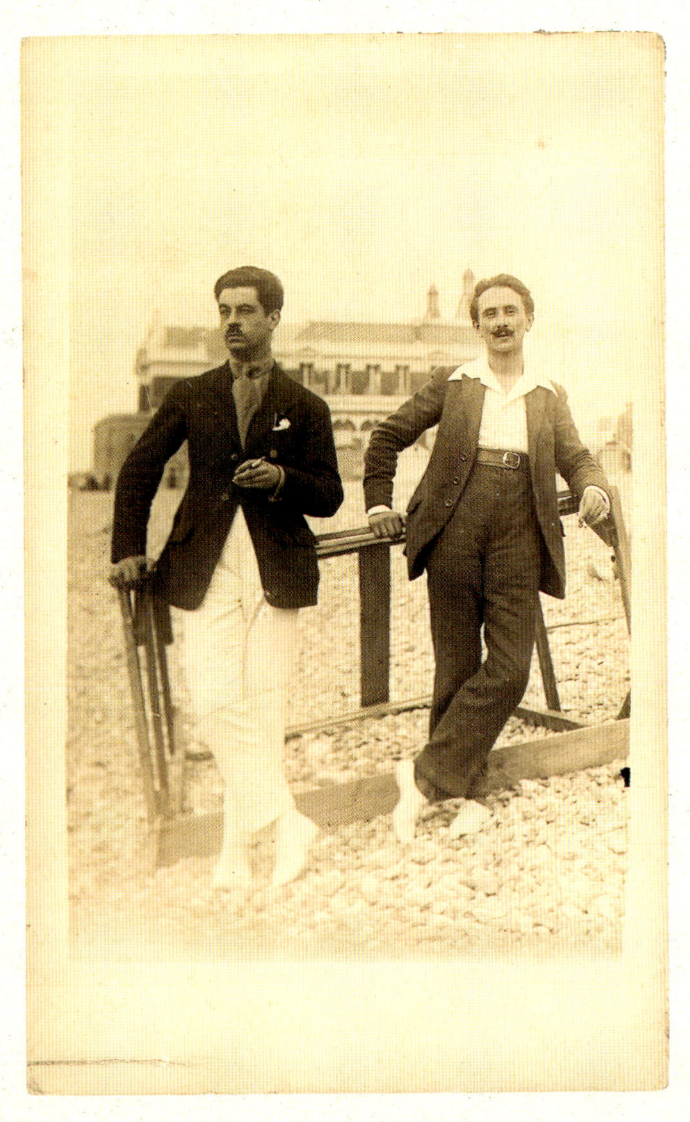

France c. 1920
< France c. 1900

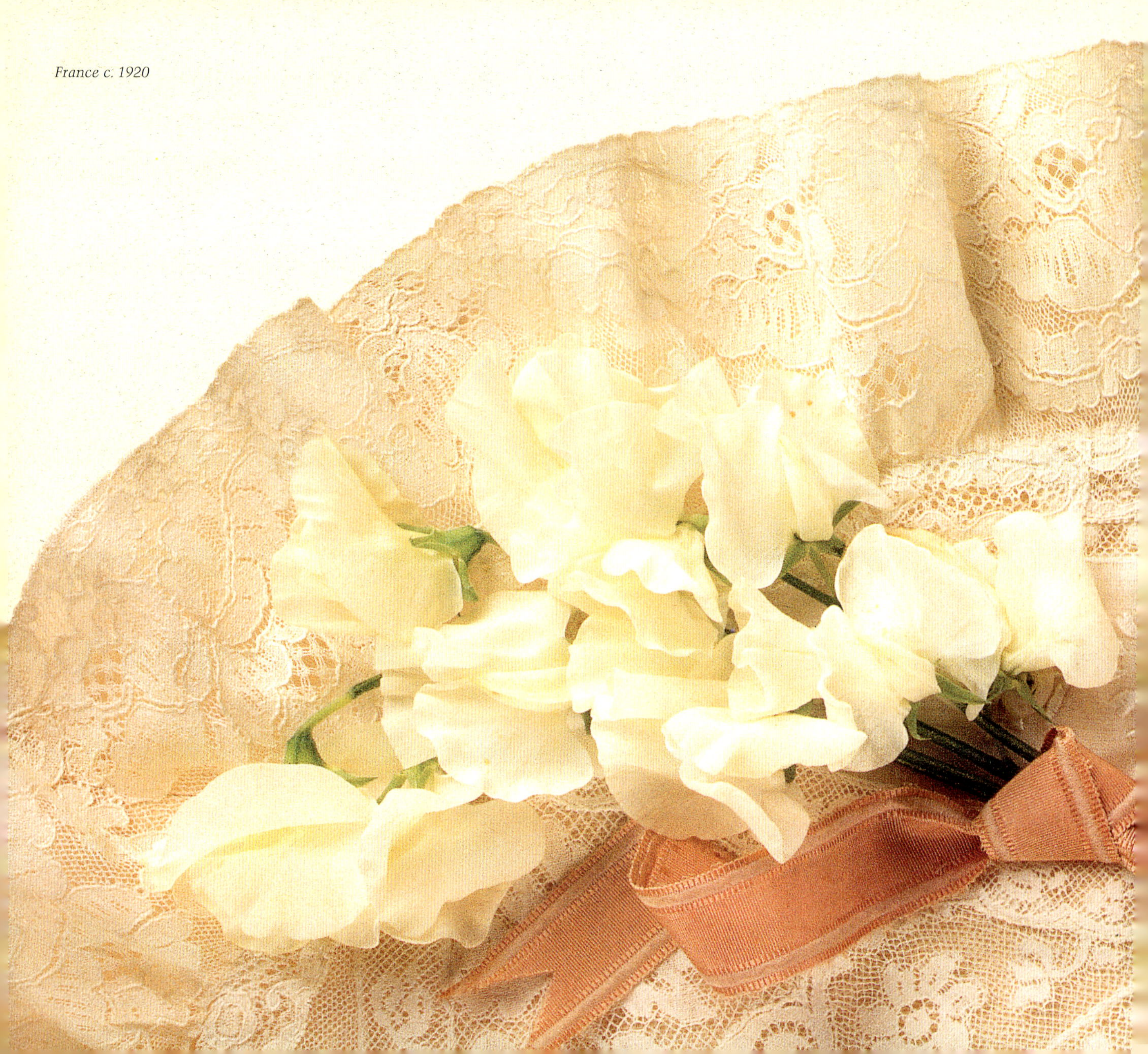

France c. 1920

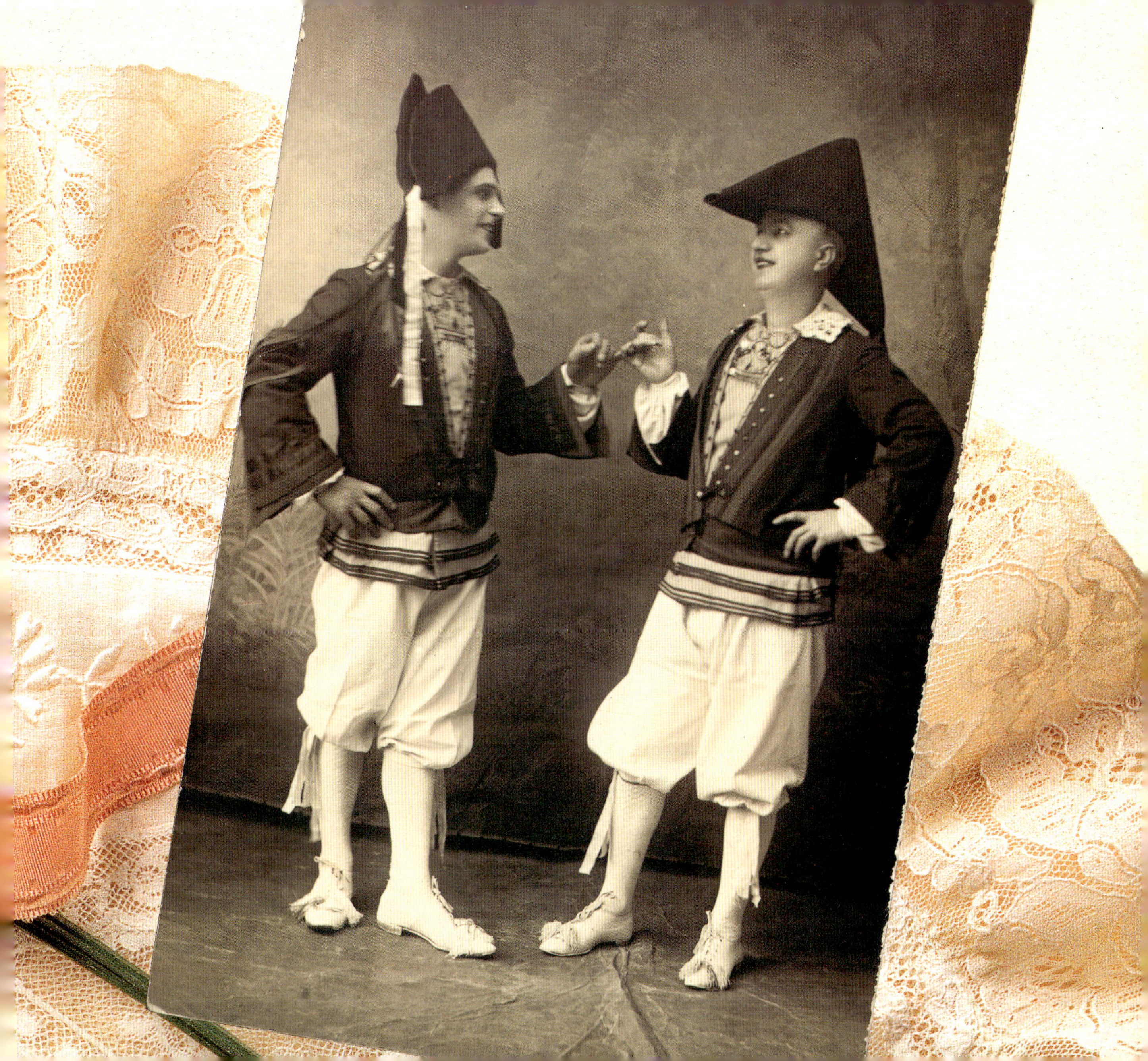

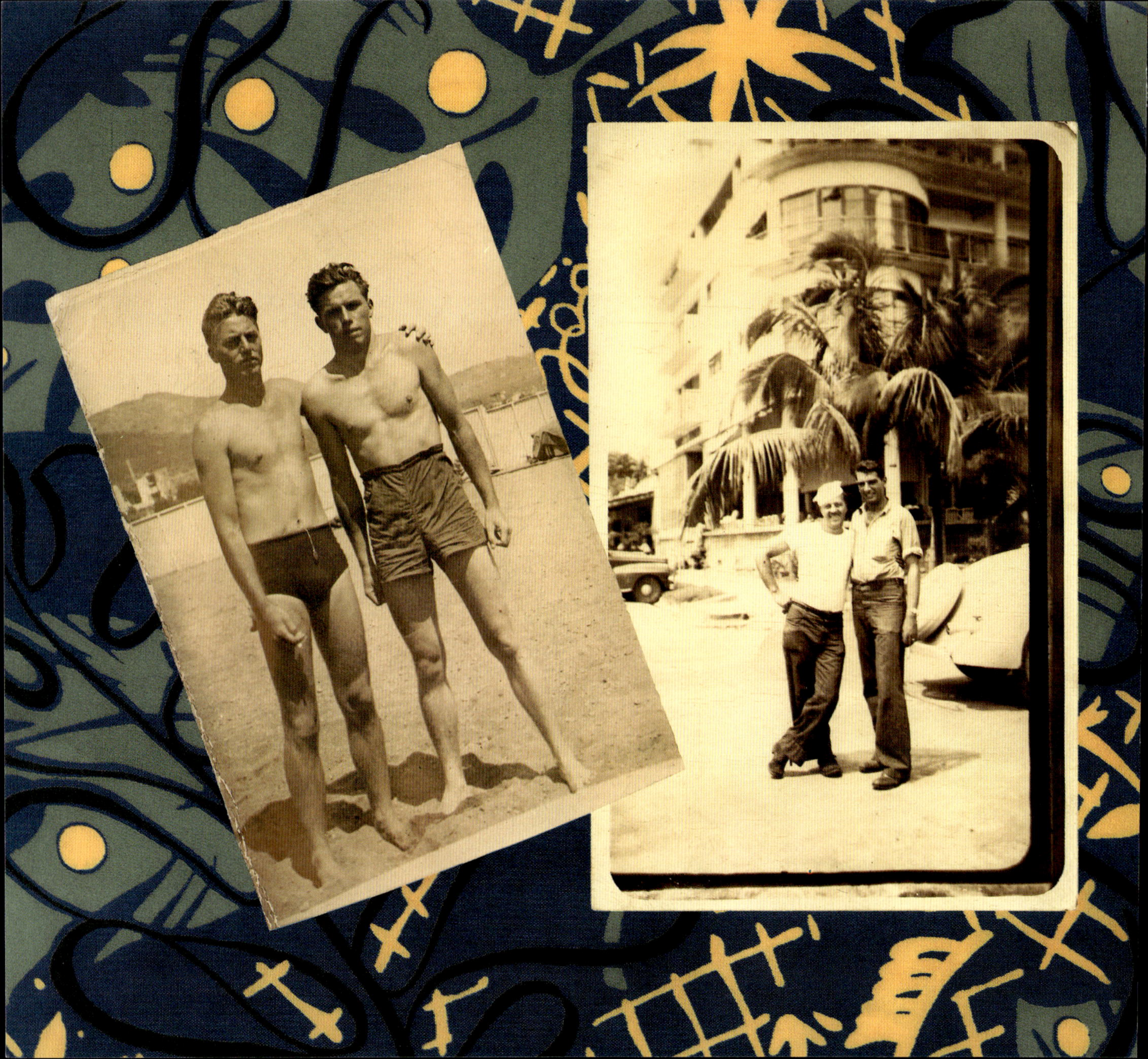

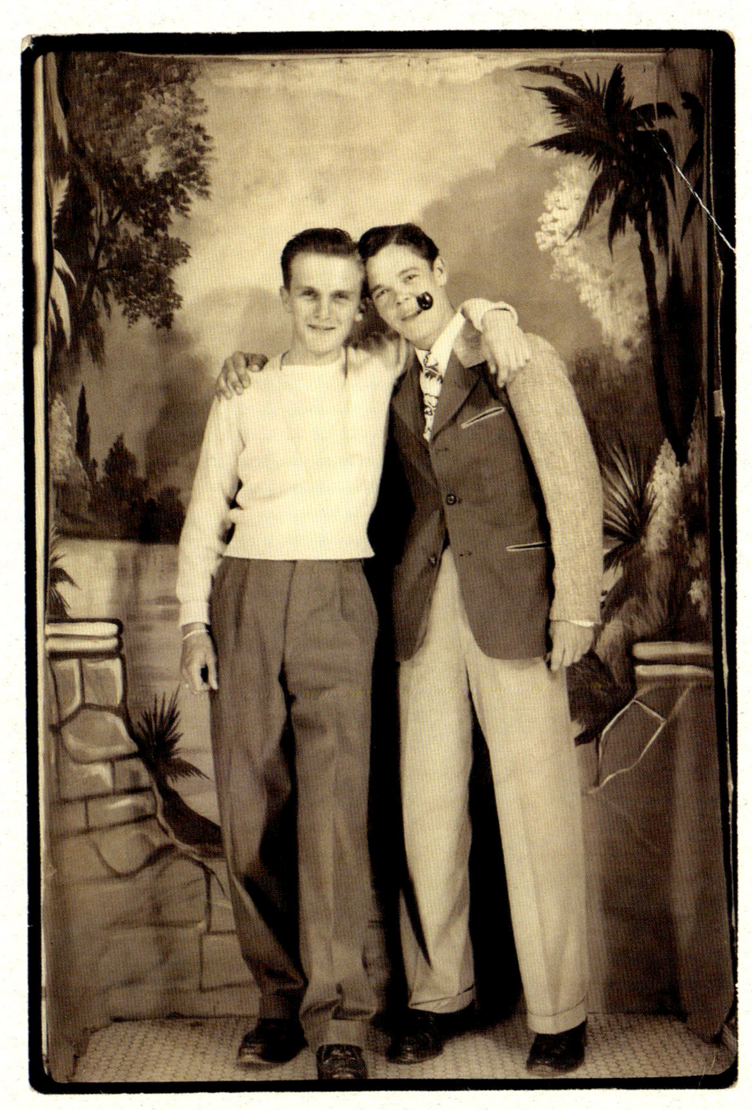

America 1947
≺ Italy 1945
≺ Mexico c. 1940

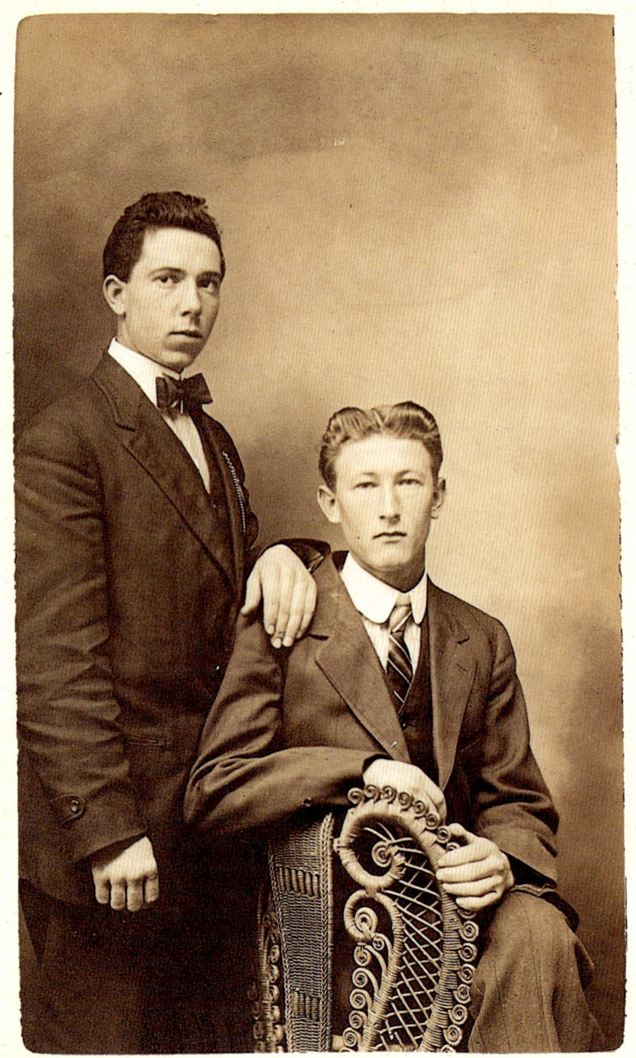

America c. 1910

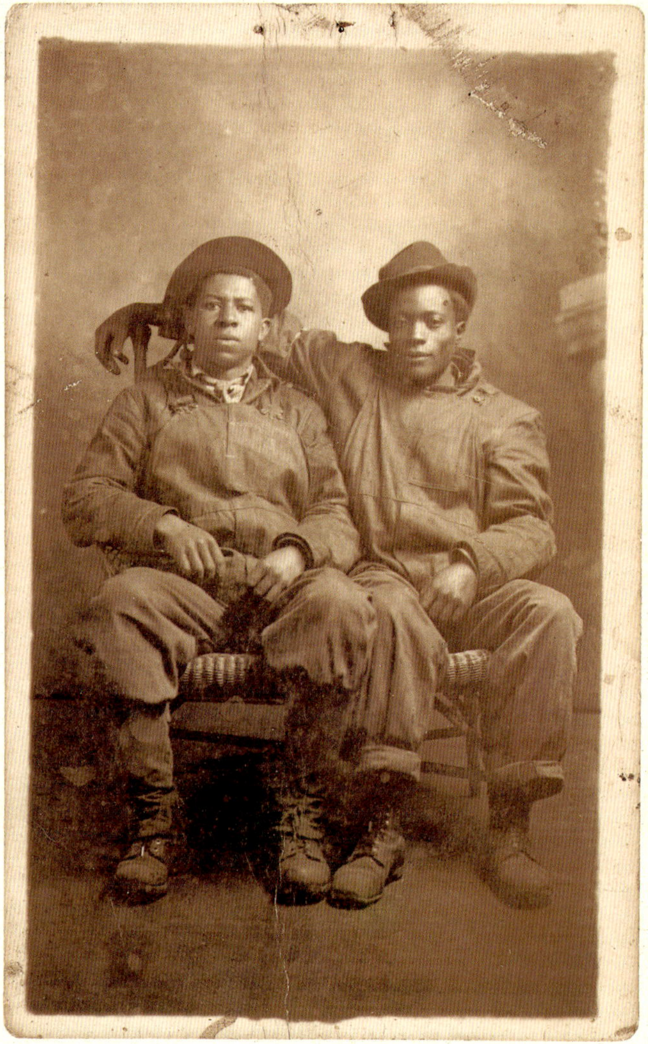

America 1910–18

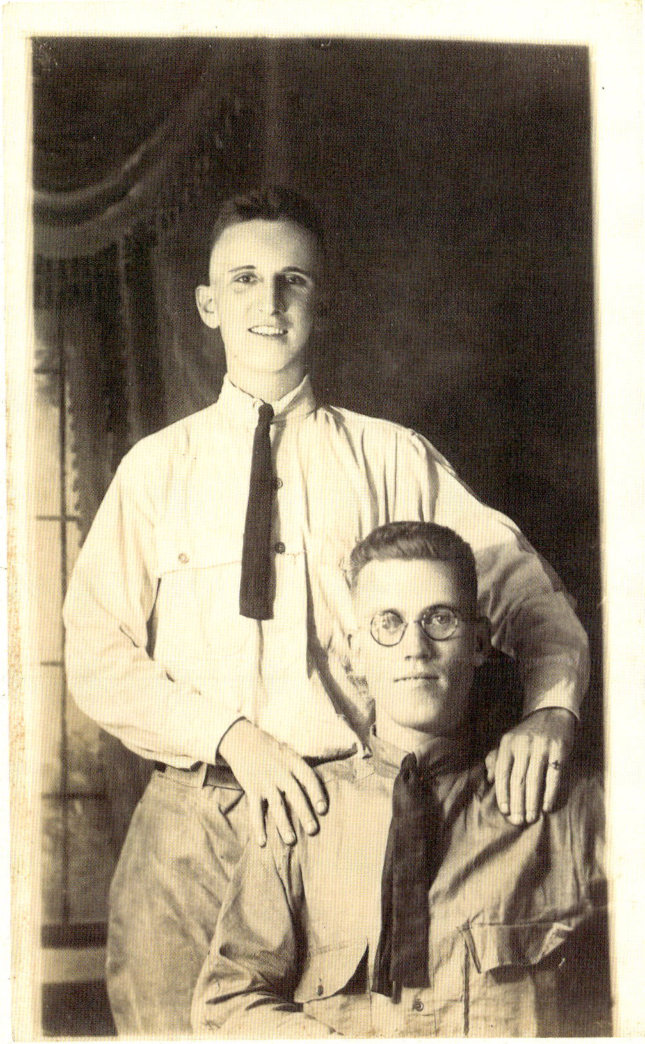

America 1918–22

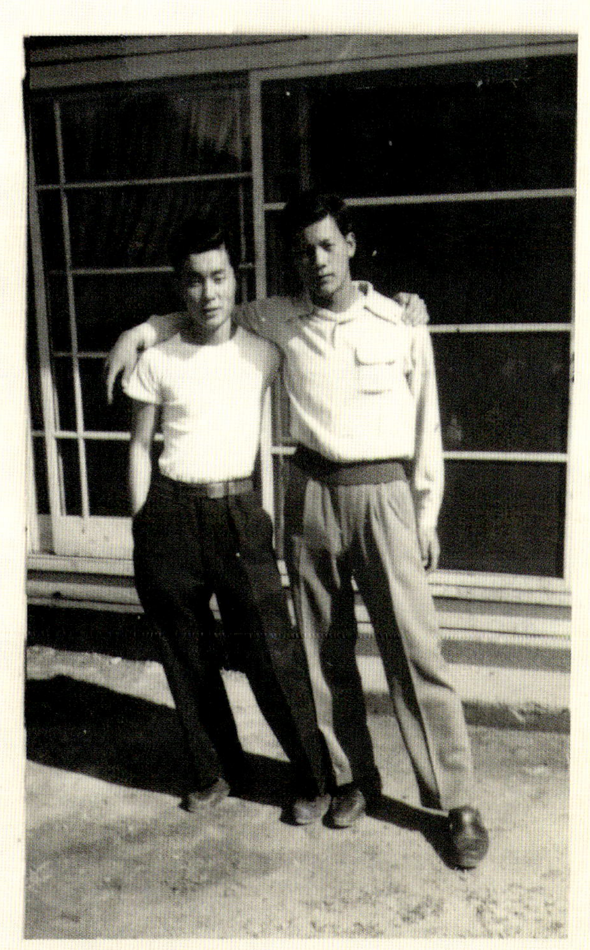

America 1940's

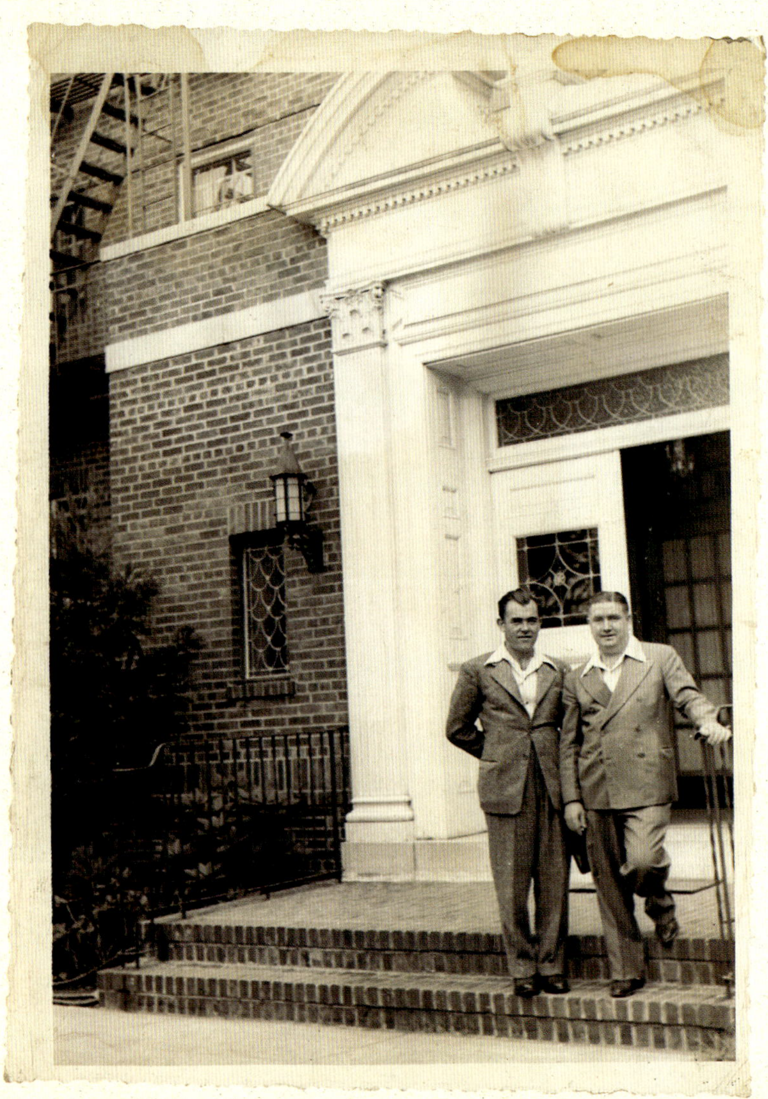

America 1940–45
America 1915–20 ➢

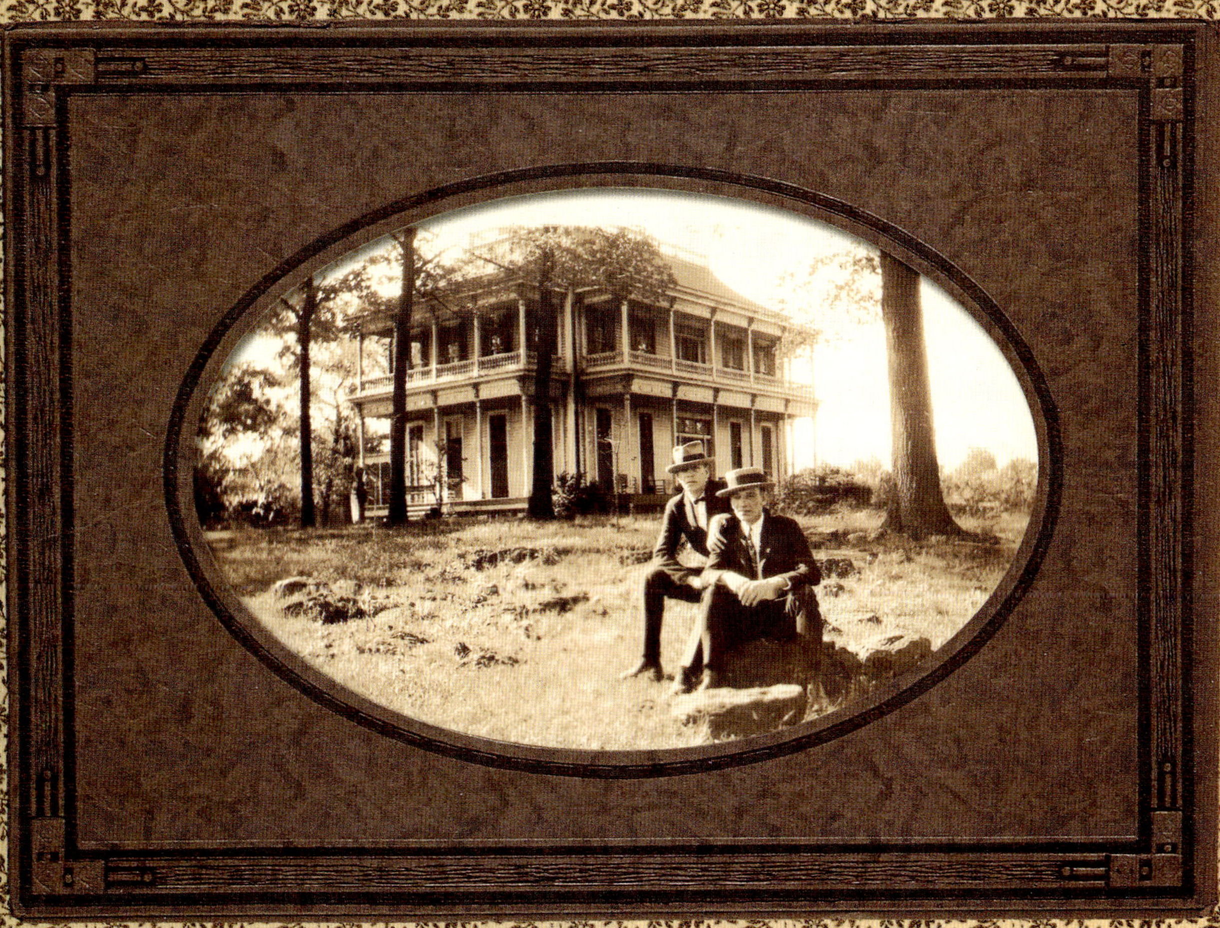

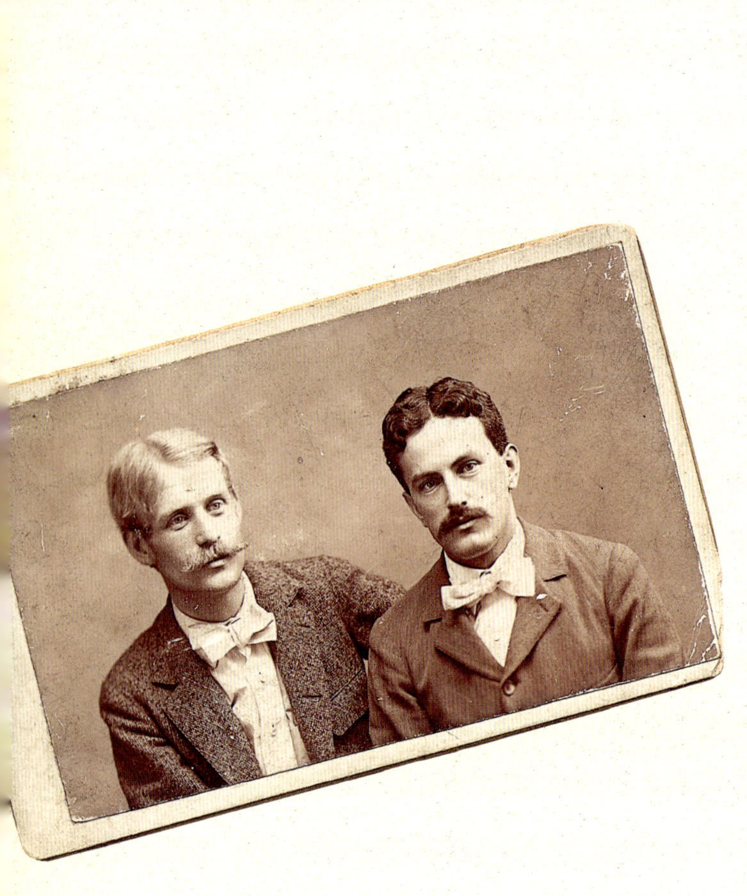

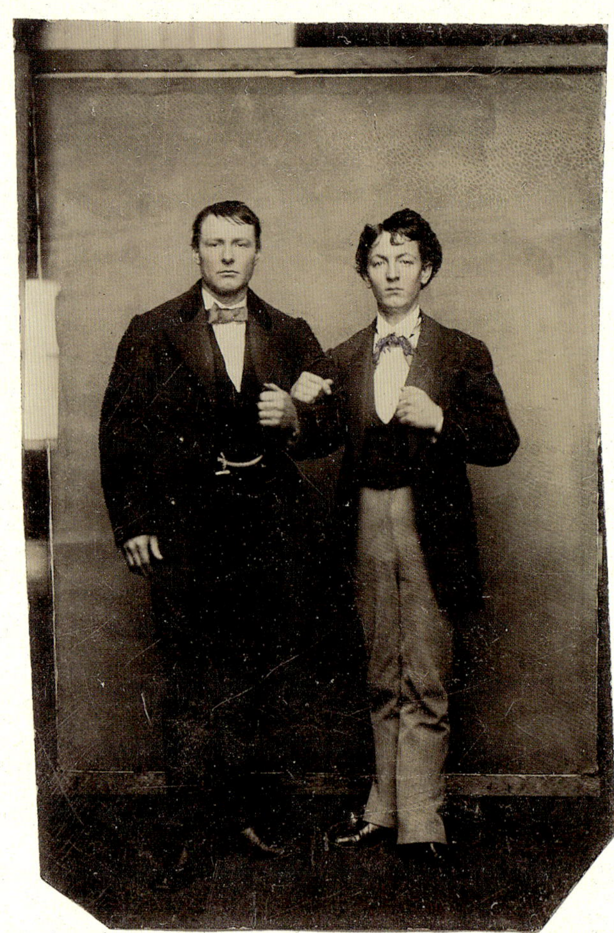

America 1890–95
America c. 1860
England c. 1900 ➤

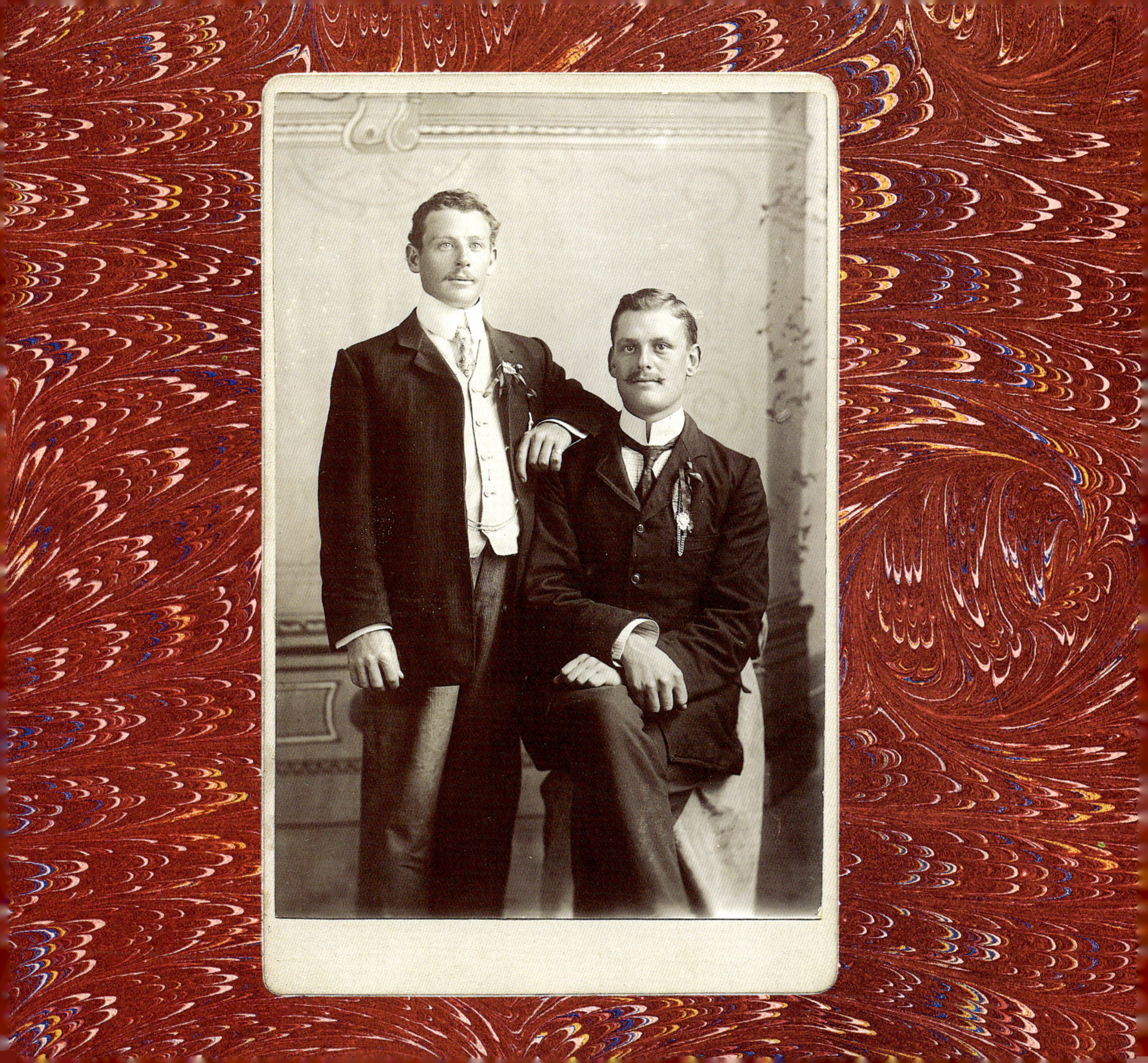

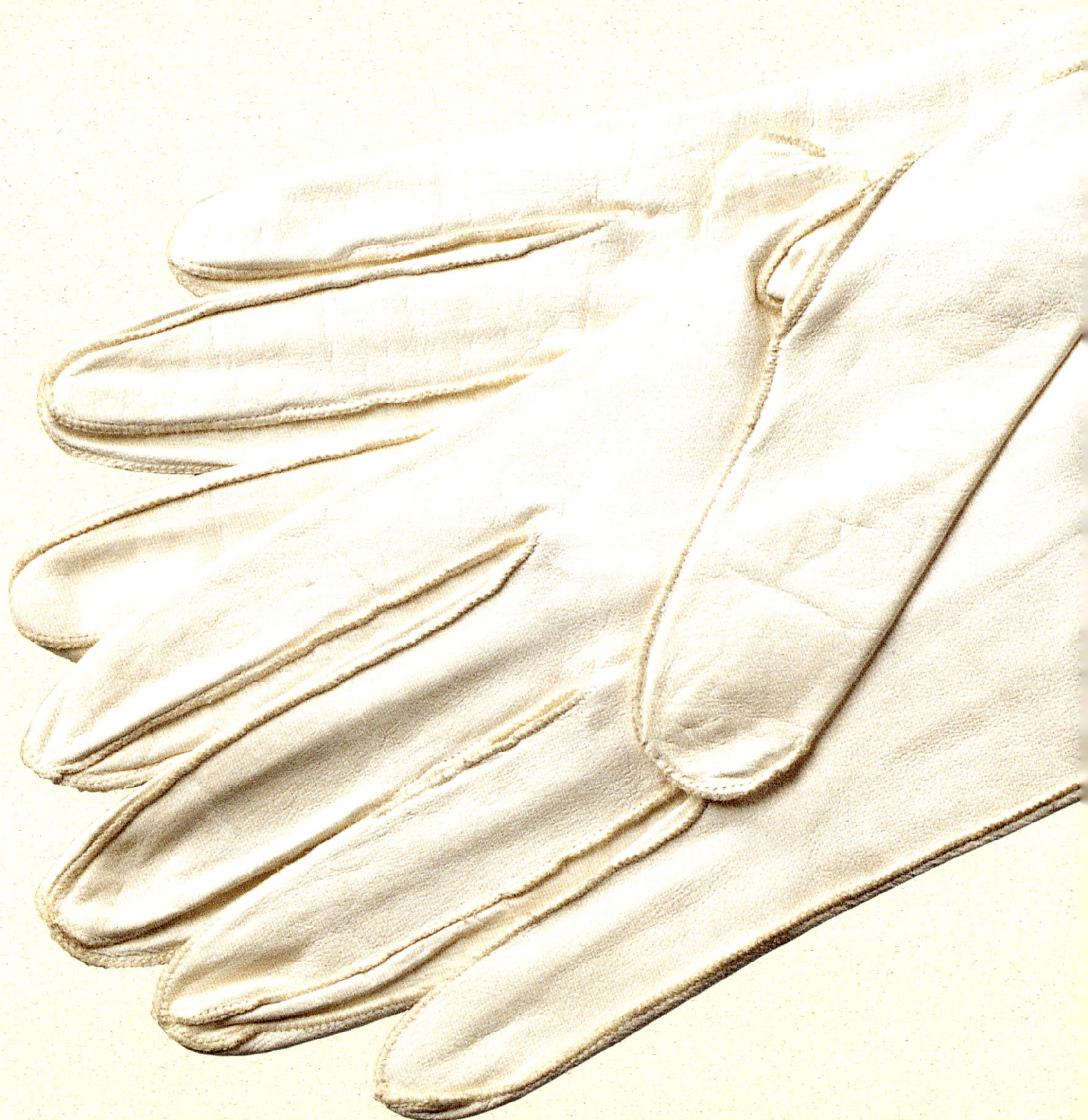

England c. 1890

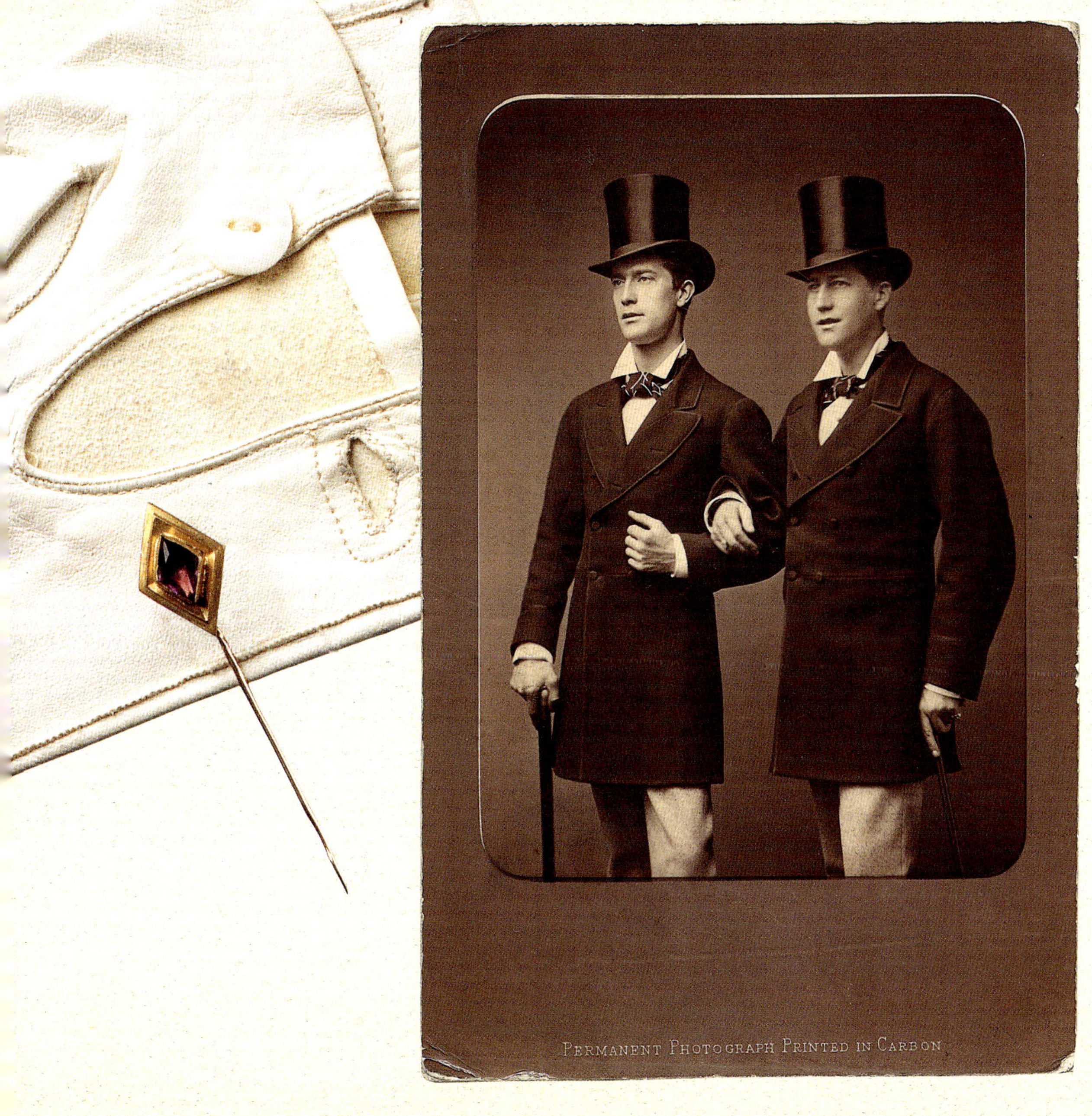
PERMANENT PHOTOGRAPH PRINTED IN CARBON

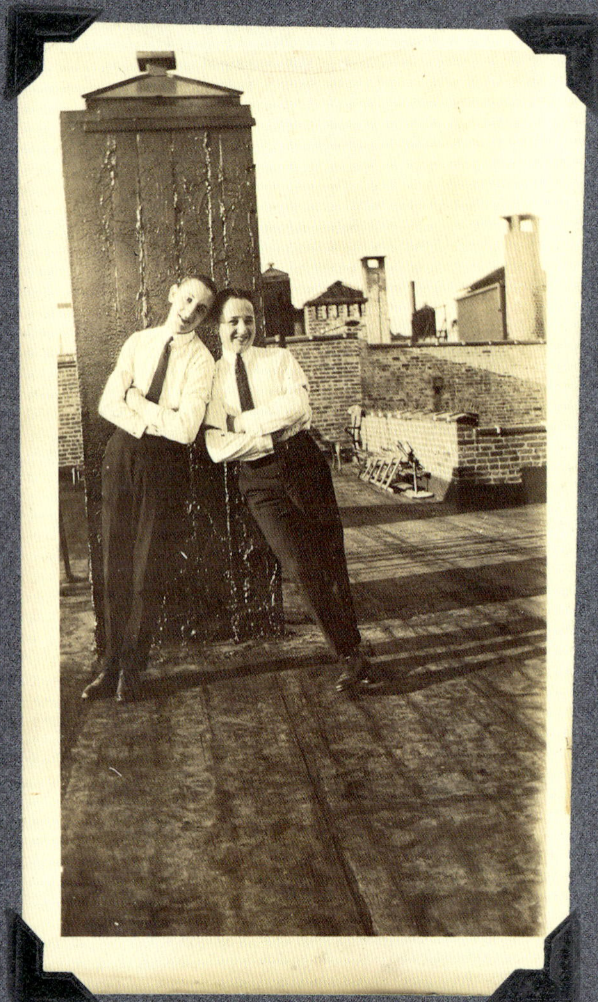

America c. 1920

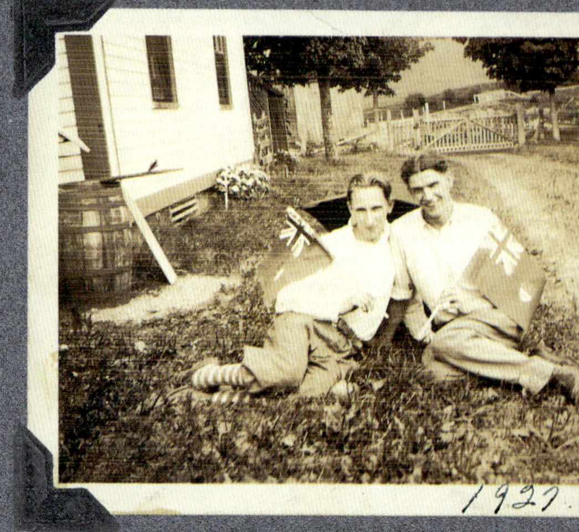

America/Canada 1927

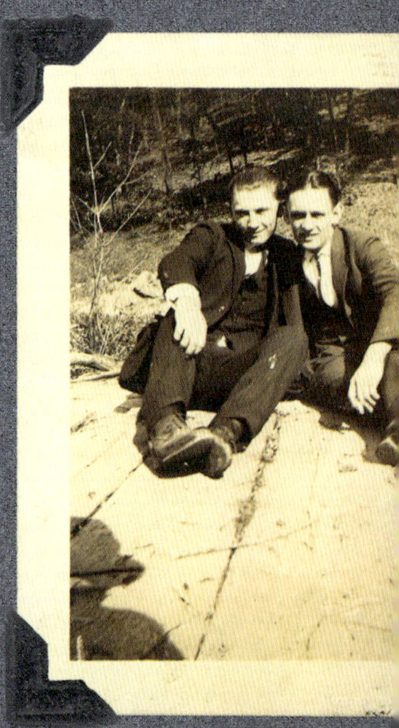

America c. 1920

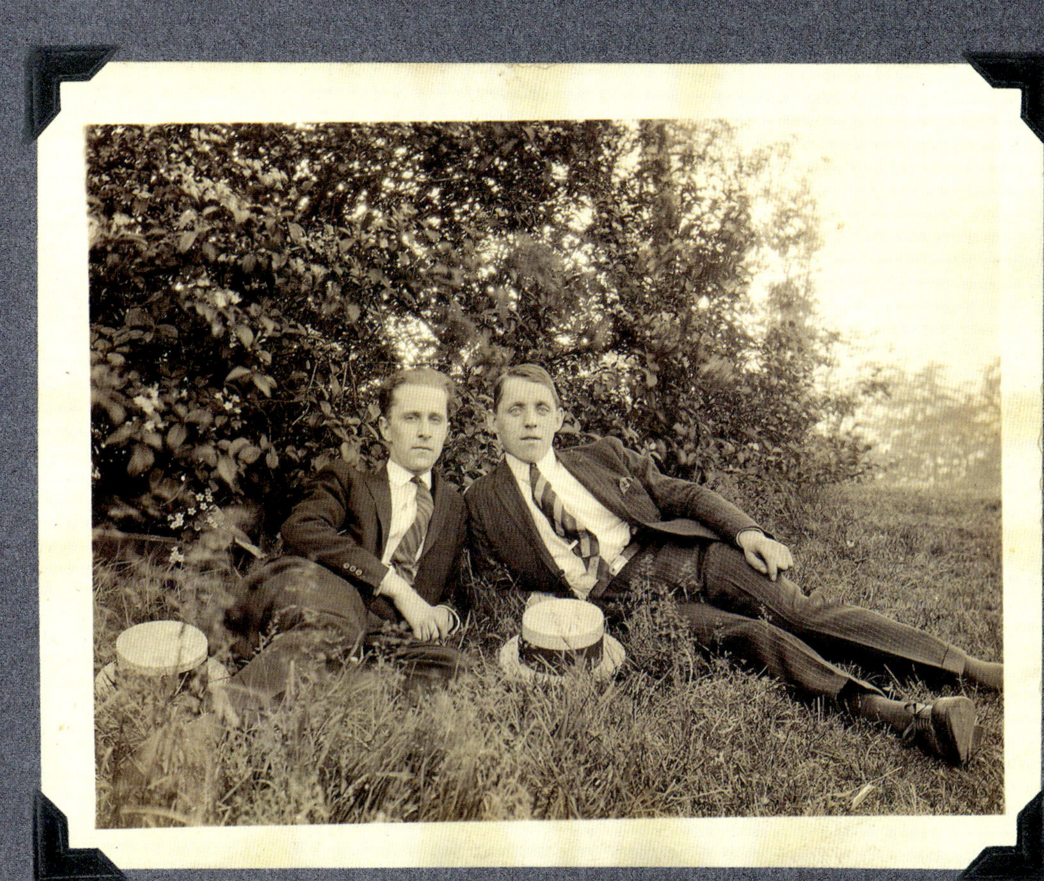

America c. 1930

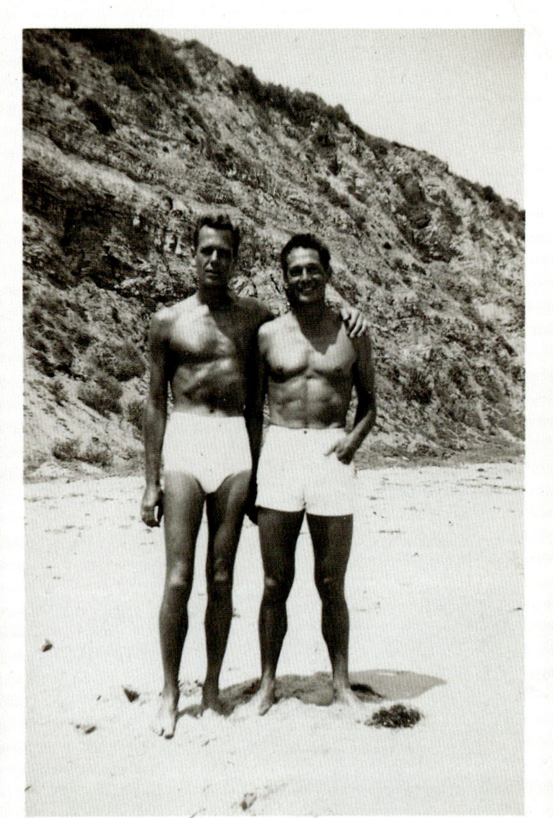

America 1950's
America 1930's
America late 1950's ➢

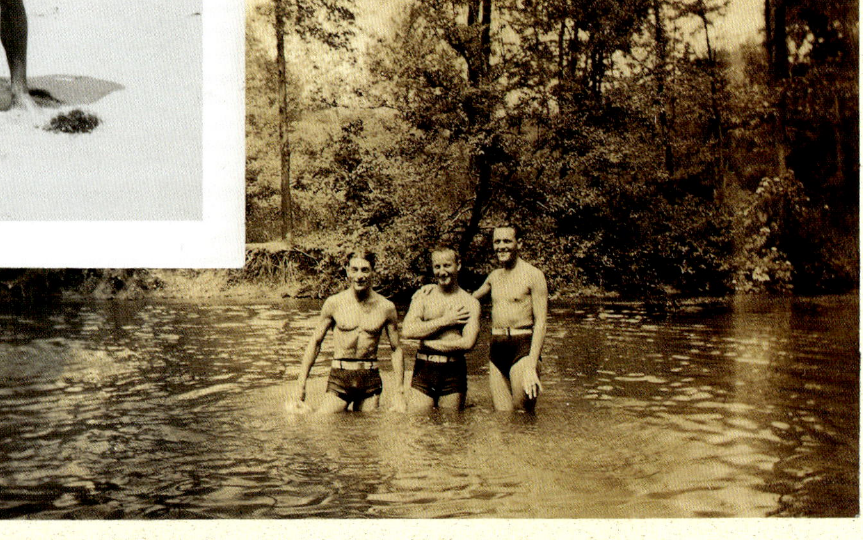

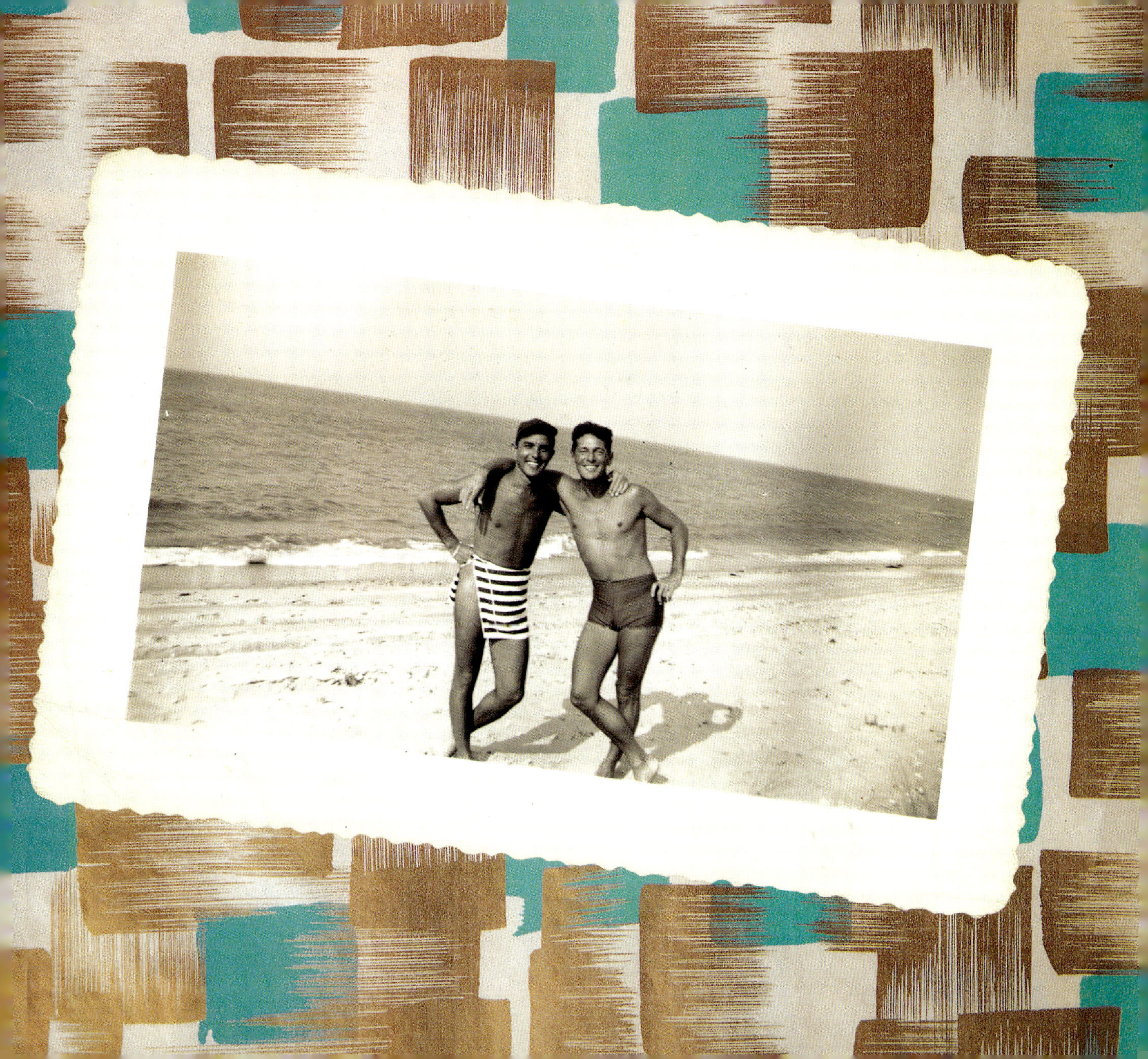

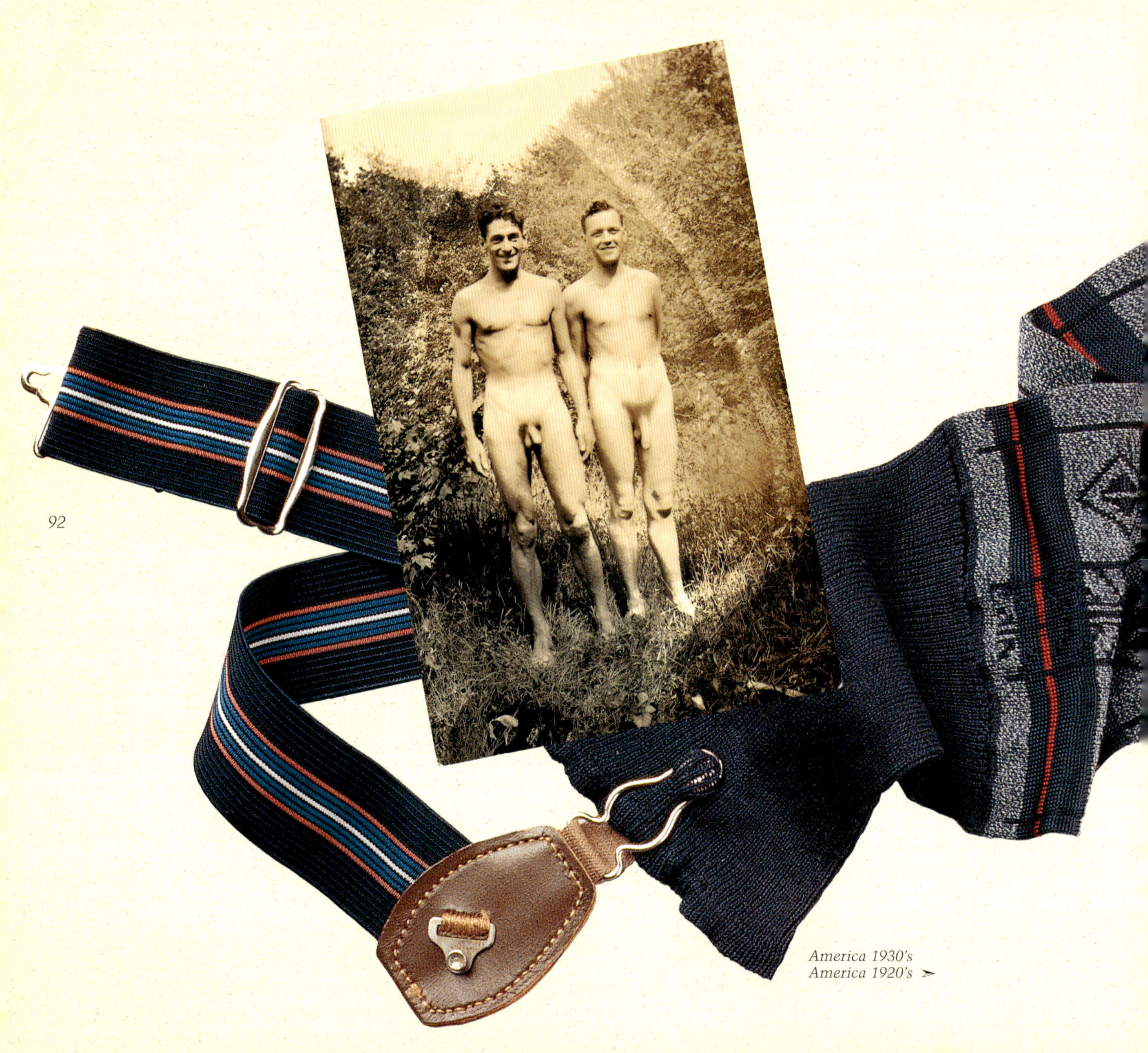

America 1930's
America 1920's ➢

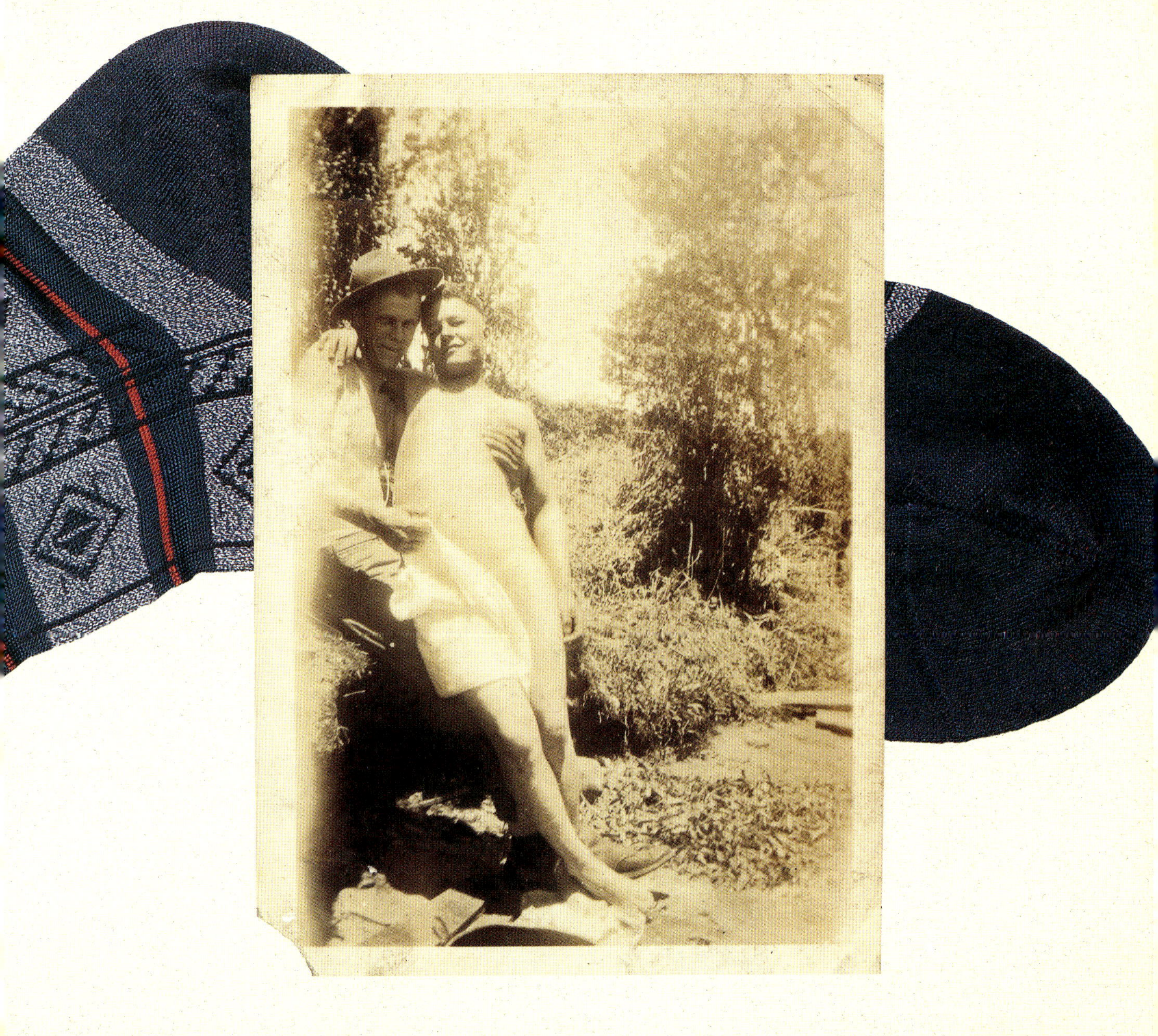

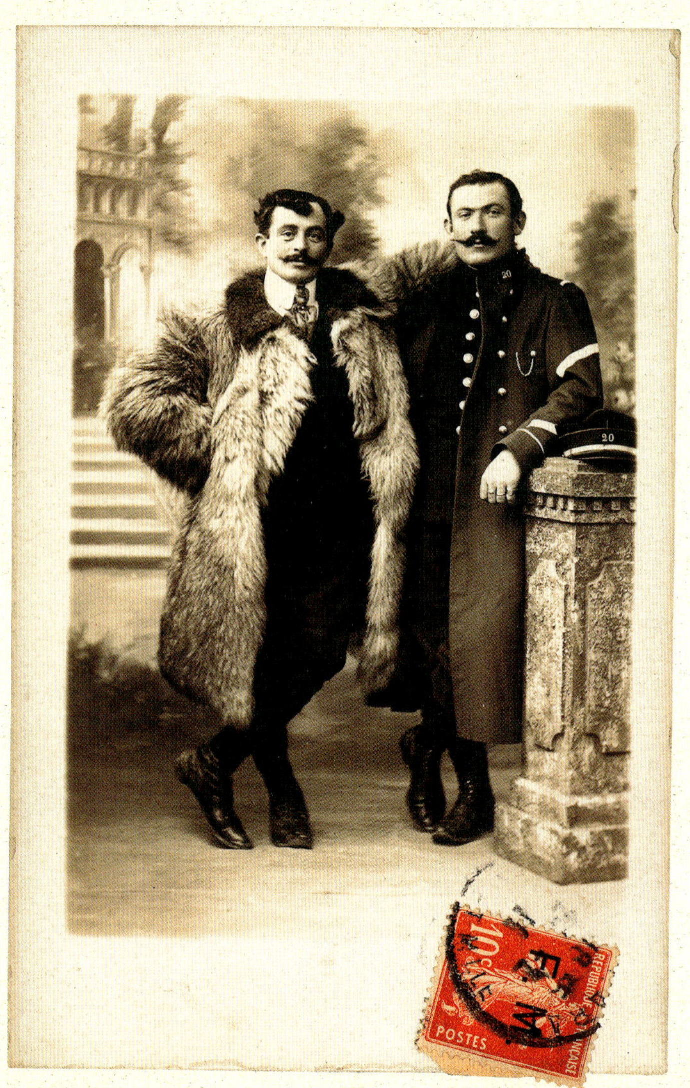

France 1911
France 1914–15 ➢

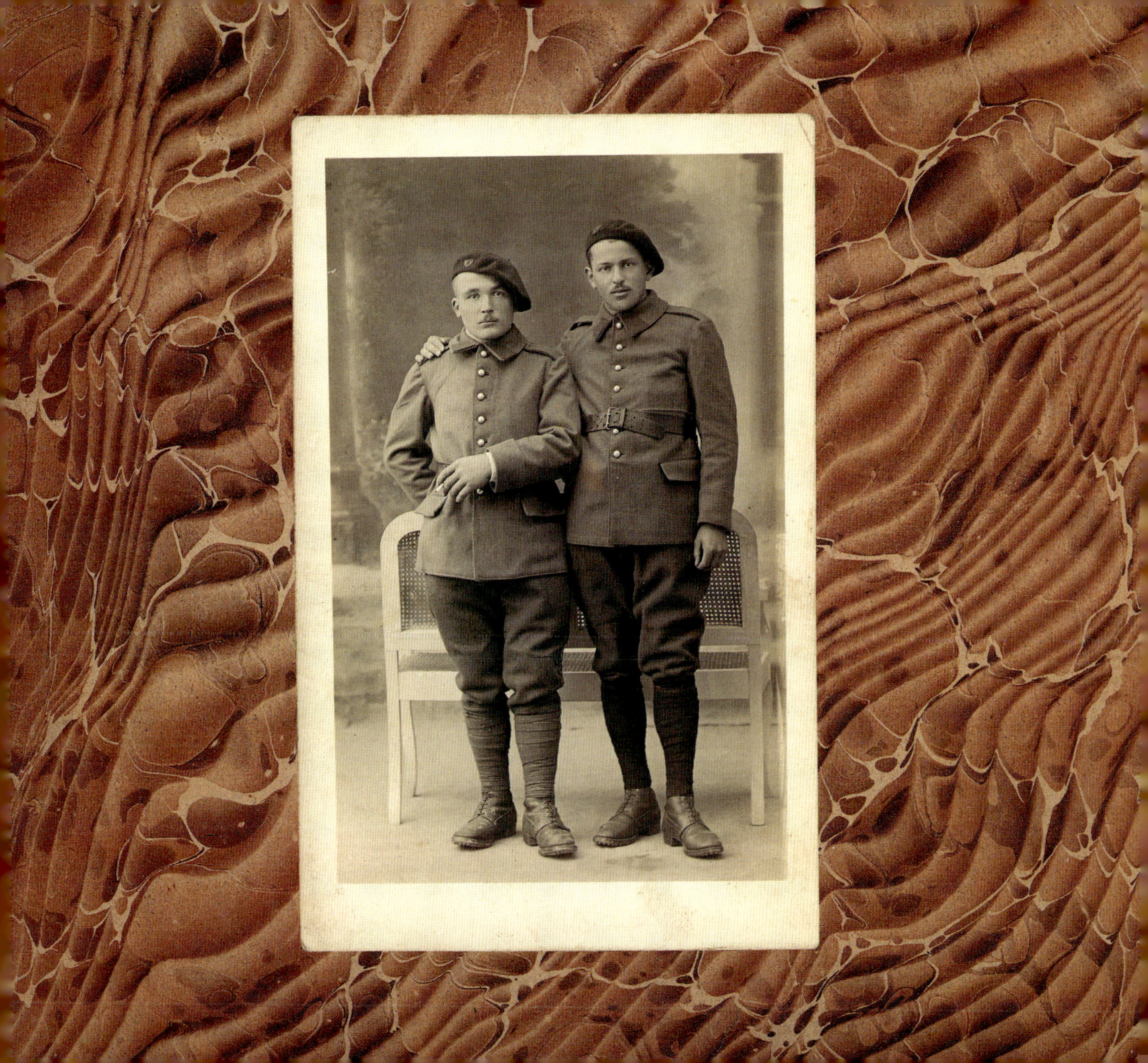

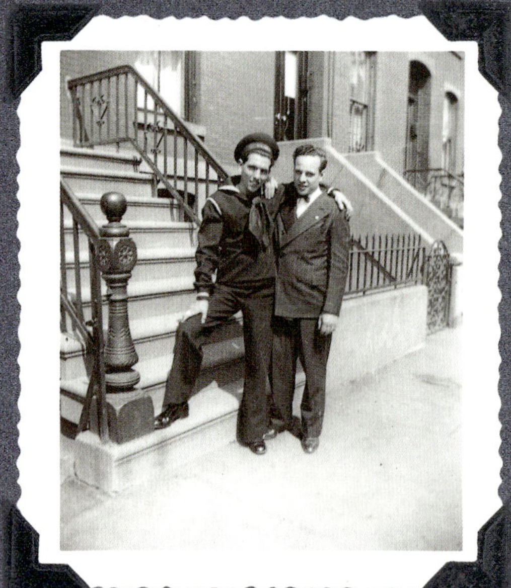

America 1941

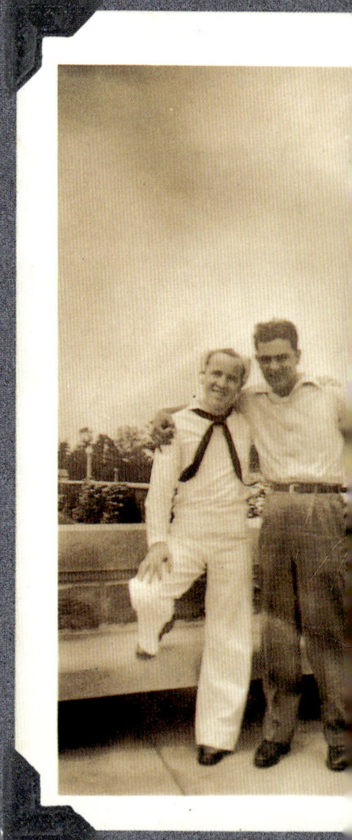

America early 1940's

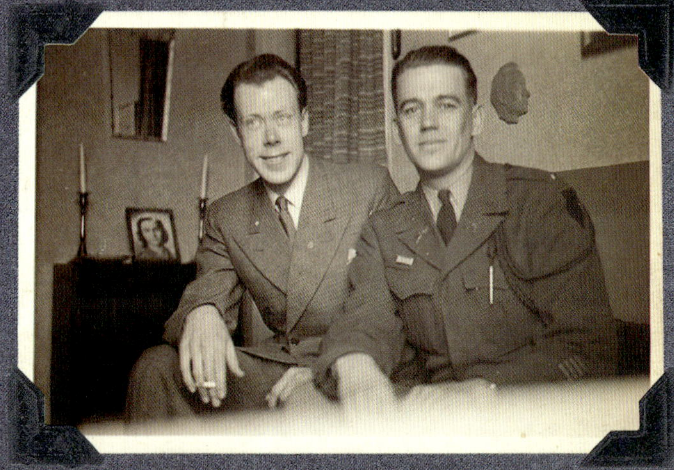

Sweden late 1940's

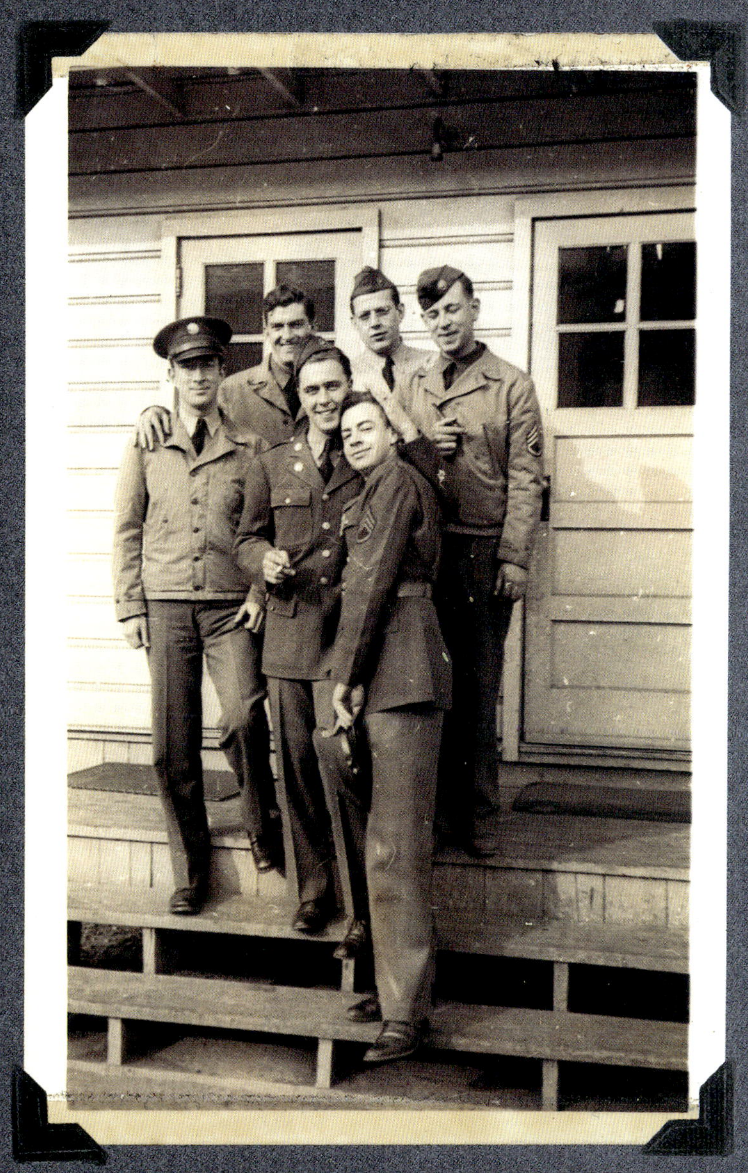

America 1941–45

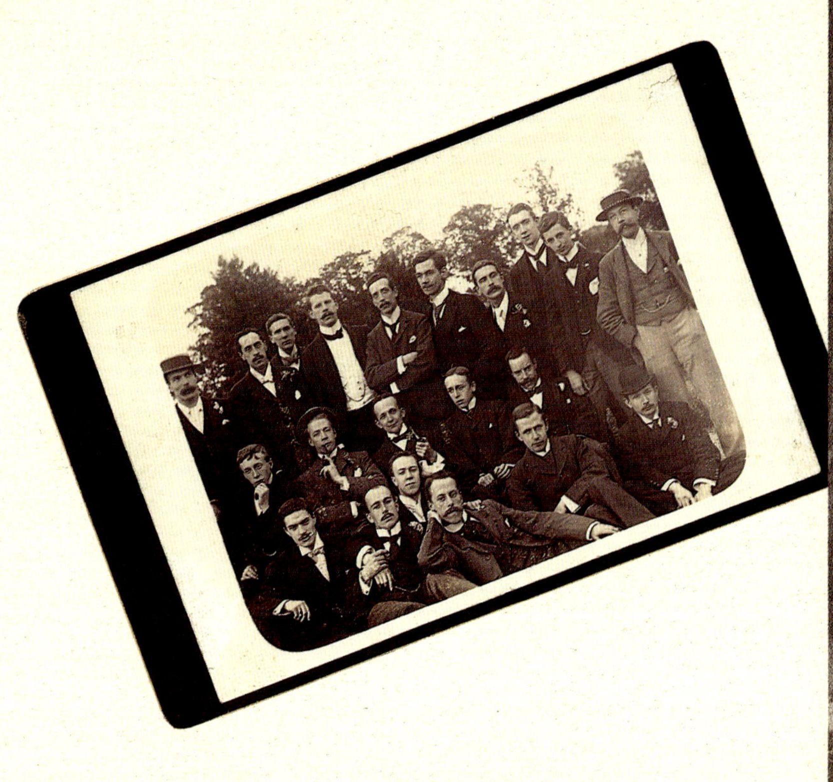

America c. 1910
America 1910–15 ➢

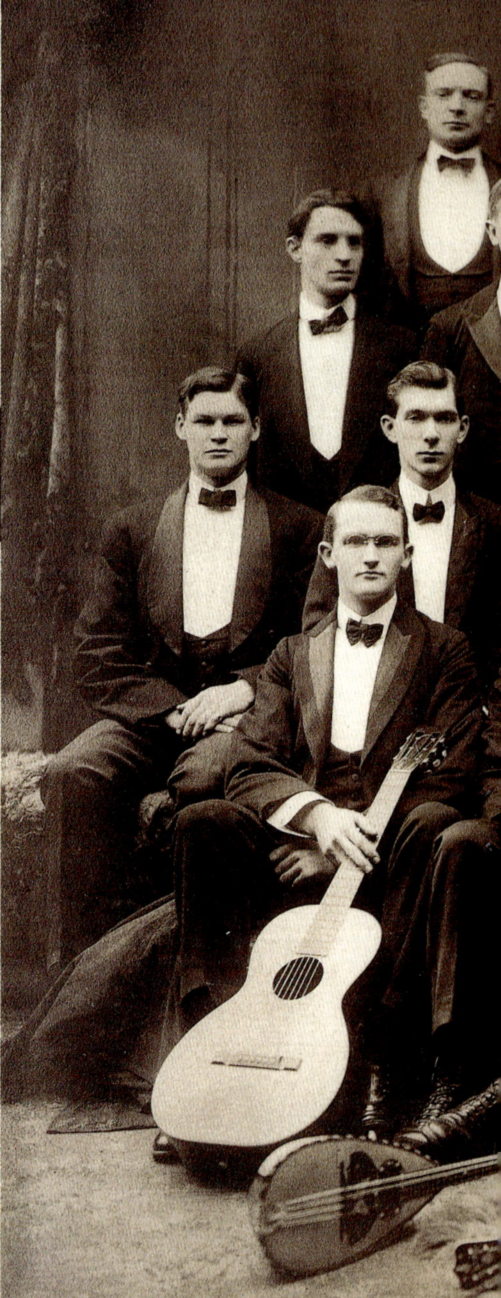

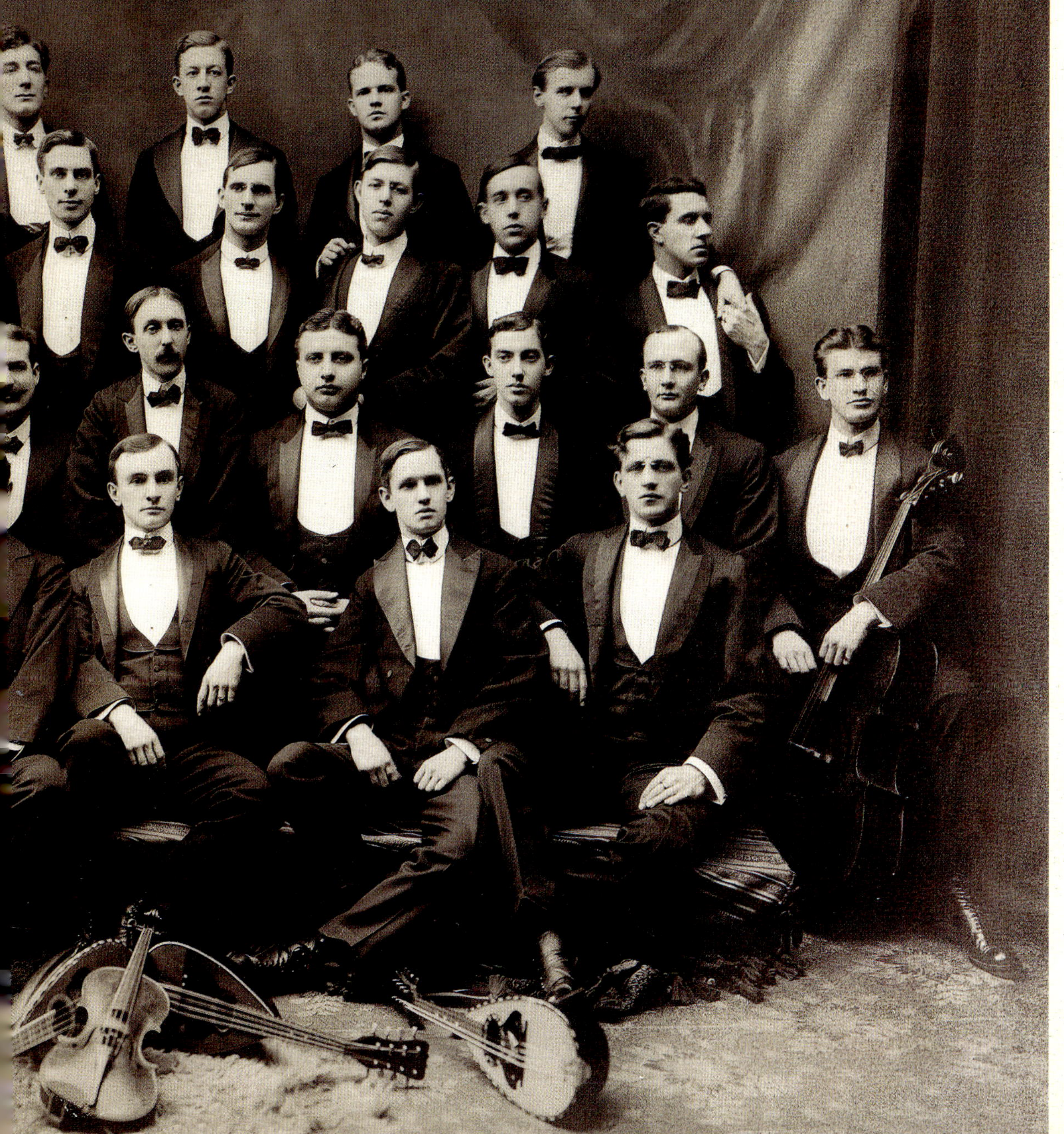

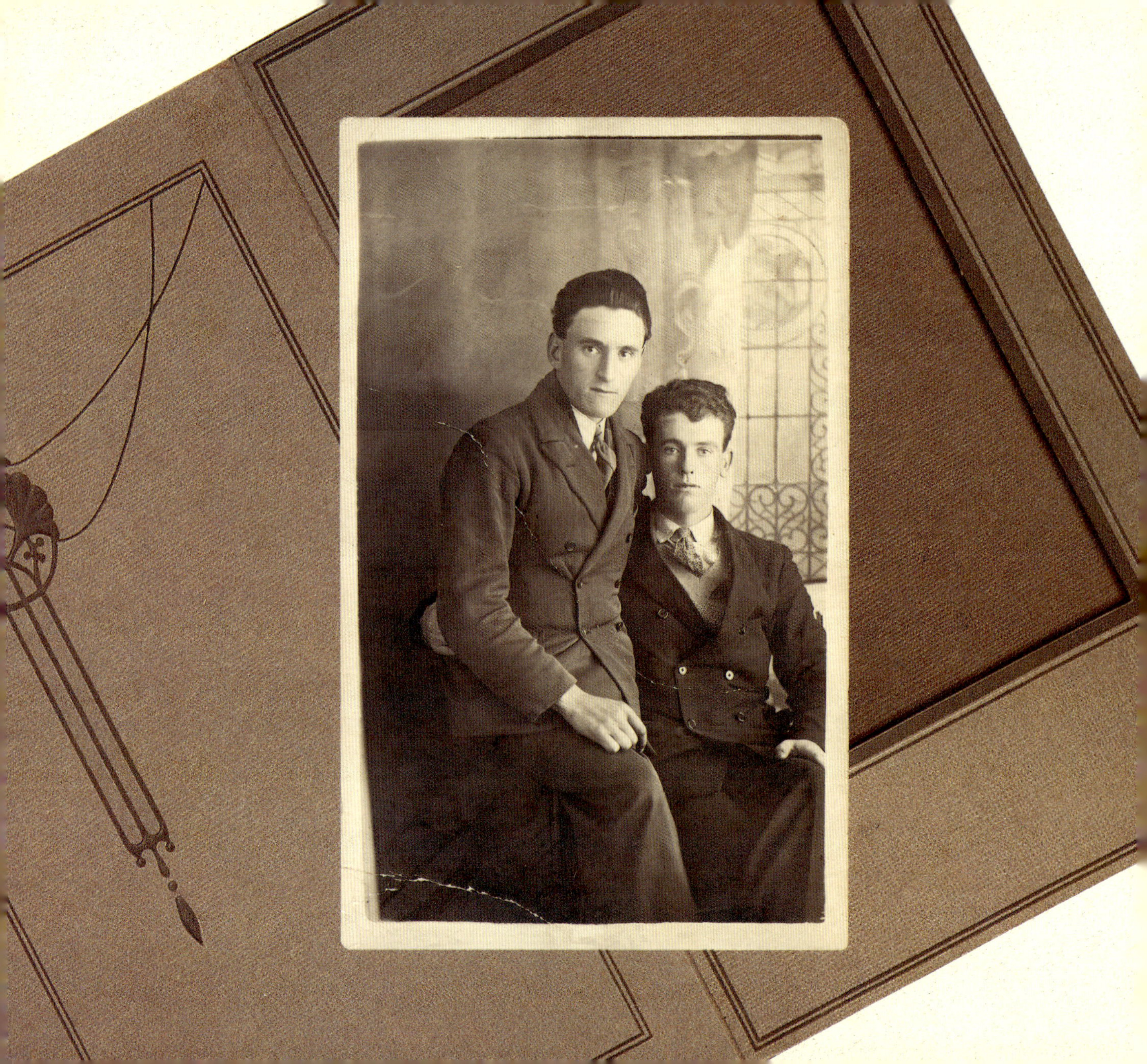

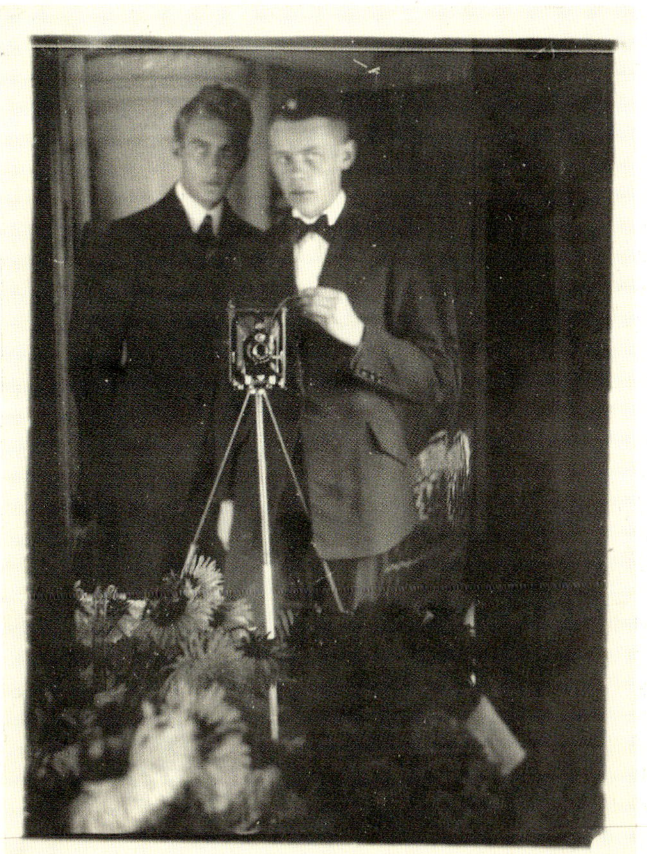

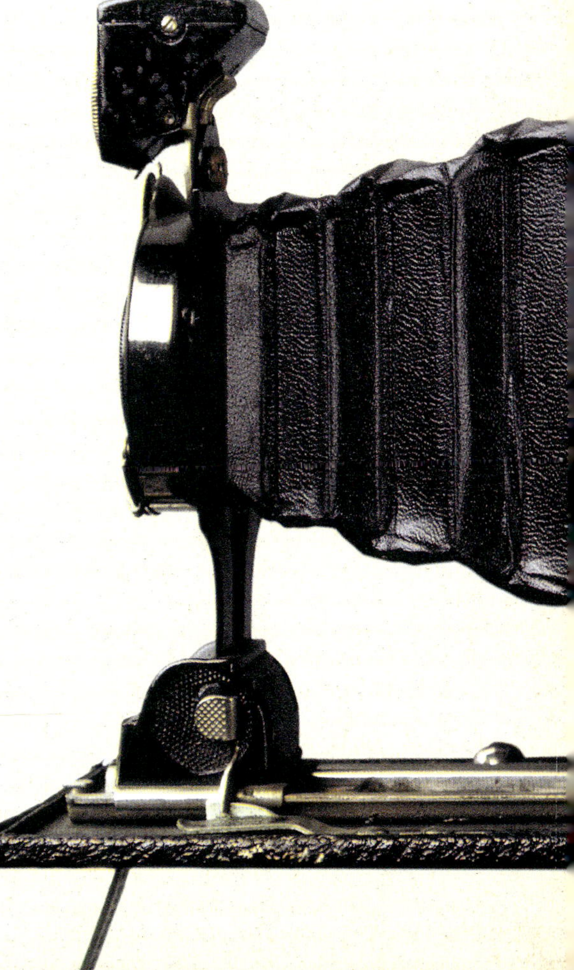

Germany 1922
America 1927

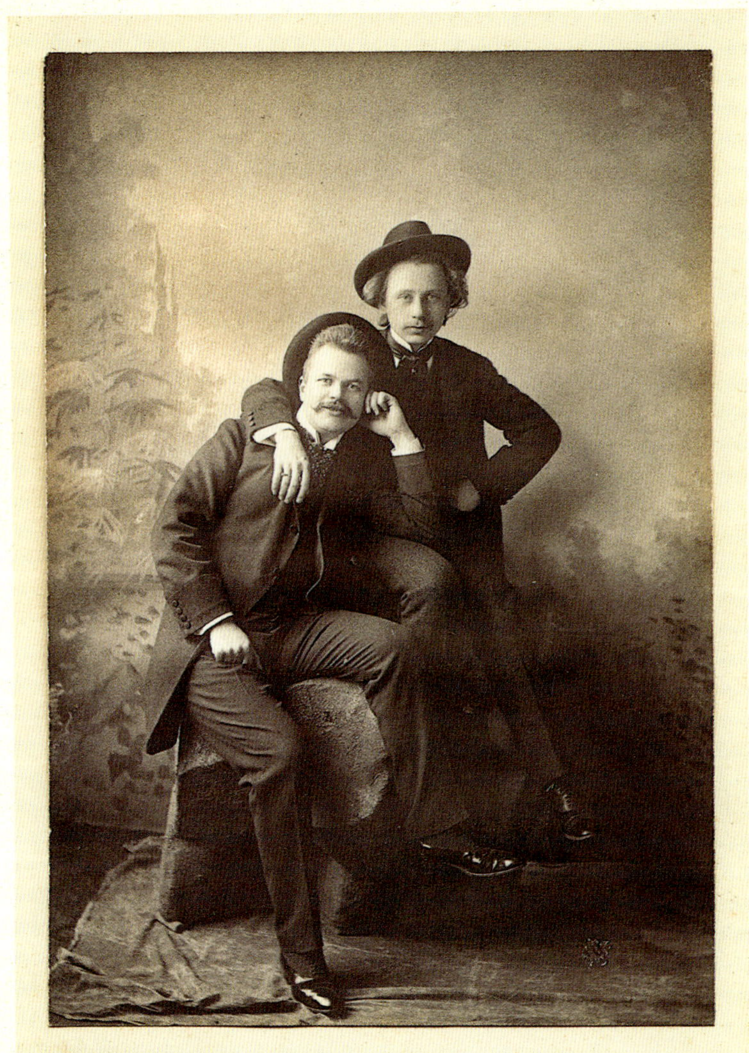

America c. 1900

Notes on the Photographs

The following abbreviations have been used to describe additional relevant details about the photographs:

DG:	Daguerreotype	AL:	Albumen paper print
AM:	Ambrotype	SG:	Silver gelatin paper print
TT:	Tintype	CC:	Cabinet card
PL:	Platinum paper print	CV:	Carte-de-visite
CB:	Carbon paper print	PC:	Postcard

Sizes are given in inches, height precedes width.
This size refers to the actual image size without borders or mounting.
Handwritten inscriptions on backs of photographs are *italicized.*
Some of the photographs in this book were digitally enhanced only for the purpose of clearer visibility.

Dust jacket: (front): America, c. 1885; TT, 3½ x 2⅝. (back) America, c. 1885; TT, 3⅞ x 2½.

Page 1: detail of p. 71. **2:** America, c. 1890; SG/CV, 2¼ x 3¾. **4:** TT, 2½ x 3⅝. **8:** America, 1911–12; TT, mounted into pin, 1″ diameter. **11:** America, 1890–95; TT, mounted into cufflinks, ½ x ⅜. **13:** DG, 3½ x 3. **14:** SG, 4½ x 2⅞. **15:** TT, 3½ x 2½. **16:** (left) SG/PC, 5½ x 3⅜. (right) SG/PC, 5½ x 3⅜, Willow Grove Park. **17:** (left) SG/PC, 5 x 3⅜. (right) SG/PC, 4¾ x 2¾. **18:** TT, 2⅛ x 1⅝. **19:** TT, 3⅜ x 2⅝. **20:** TT, 3⅜ x 2⅜. **21:** TT, 3⅜ x 2¼. **22:** (left) SG, 4¼ x 2½. (right) SG, 2⅛ x 3⅛. **24:** SG/CC, 5½ x 3¾. **25:** SG/PC, 4¾ x 3⅛ , *April 10th '15.* **26:** TT, 4 x 2½. **27:** (left) SG/PC, 5$\frac{7}{16}$ x 3½. *Zoppot 10/9, 1913* (Zoppot—now Sopot—is presently part of Poland). (right) TT, 3½ x 2½. **28:** (left) SG, 4 x 2$\frac{5}{16}$. (right) SG, 3⅛ x 2. **29:** SG/PC (trimmed), 3⅛ x 2⅛. **30:** SG, 2½ x 1¾. **31:** SG, 2⅜ x 1⅝. **32:** (left) AL/CC, 5$\frac{13}{16}$ x 3⅞, *13 December 1896.* (right) SG/PC, 5½ x 3½, (front) with an Arab chum. (back) *9 November 1912 I have had the opportunity to see Mr. Petit, he was charming. He and Mr. Petit told me to send you their best wishes, And this frontier of* (illegible)? *I thank you for your cards. Barrack-life is always charming. Cordial handshake. Please give me Pierre Yves's address* (translated from the French). **33:** (left) SG/PC, 4$\frac{11}{16}$ x 2⅞, *London, 1910, Sept.* (right) SG/CC, 5¾ x 3$\frac{15}{16}$. **34:** TT, 3½ x 2⅜. **35:** TT, 3$\frac{5}{16}$ x 2¼.

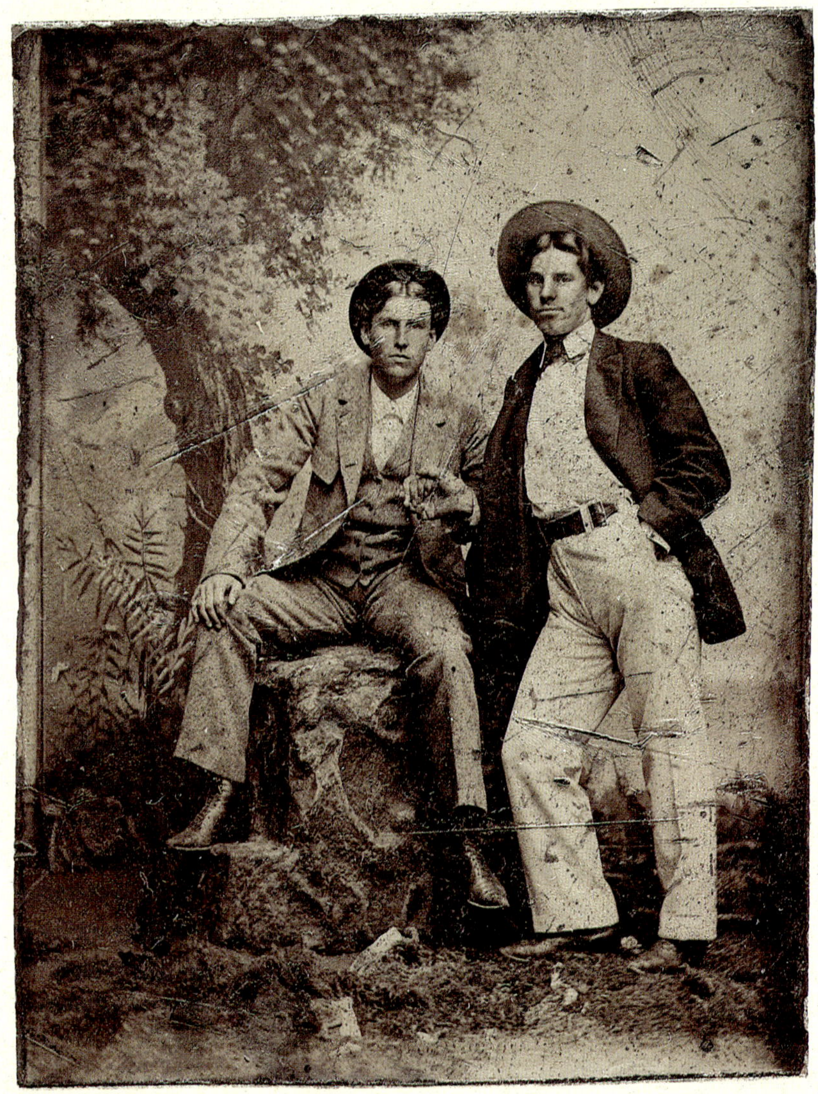

America 1870's

36: (top) SG/PC, 3⅜ x 5½. (bottom) SG/PC, 3⅛ x 5. **37:** SG, 7⅜ x 5, *December 2, 1951.* **38:** AM, 2¼ x 2⅝. **39:** SG/PC, 5⅜ x 3⅜. **40:** SG/PC, 3⅛ x 4¼, *with fond memories of a* (illegible), *Strasbourg, Königsberg, 1914–15* (translated from the German). **41:** SG, 2⅜ x 3⅛. **42:** (left) SG, 5 3/16 x 3 3/16. (right) SG, 4¼ x 2⅜. **43:** SG, 4⅛ x 2⅜. **44:** SG/PC, 3¼ x 2¾, Atlantic City Souvenir, *After taking a dip in the Bloody Hocean* (sic). **45:** SG/CV, 3⅜ x 2¼. **47:** SG/PC, 3½ x 5½. **48:** TT, 3⅜ x 2½. **49:** TT, 3½ x 2½. **50:** (left) SG/PC, 5⅜ x 3⅜. (right) SG/PC, 4⅛ x 3. **51:** SG/PC, 5½ x 3½. **52:** TT, 1½ x 1⅛. **53:** TT, 1⅝ x 1⅛. **54:** AL/CV, 3 13/16 x 2 5/16. **55:** SG/PC, 5 3/16 x 3⅛, *taken 11/27/15, Petersburg, Va.* **56:** SG, 4⅛ x 2⅜. **57:** SG, 3⅛ x 2⅛, stamped: 1935 Apr 30. **59:** SG/CC, 5½ x 3¾. **60:** SG/PC, 4 x 3⅛, Niagara Falls Souvenir. **61:** SG, 2⅞ x 4¼. **62:** (left) SG, 6¾ x 5, *Me, Aug, 1936.* (right) SG, 4⅛ x 2⅜. **63:** (left) SG, 4⅛ x 2½. (right) SG, 3 1/16 x 2, *July 6, 1938.* **64:** AM, 2¾ x 2⅛. **65:** SG/PC, 5¼ x 3¼, *To Father from Wild West.* **66:** (left) SG, 4½ x 3⅛. (right) SG, 4½ x 1¾. **67:** (left) SG/PC, 4⅛ x 2½. (right) SG/PC, 5⅜ x 3⅜. **68:** (left) SG, 4⅛ x 2⅜. (right) SG, 4¼ x 2¼. **69:** SG, 2½ x 1½. **70:** SG/CC, 5½ x 3⅞, *1895 Xmas.* **71:** SG/PC, 4 x 3. **72:** TT, 3⅝ x 2⅜. **73:** SG/PC, 5¼ x 3¼. **74:** SG/PC, 5½ x 3½. **75:** SG/PC, 4½ x 3. **77:** SG/PC, 5½ x 3½, *to our little comrade and ally* (translated from the French). **78:** (left) SG, 3⅛ x 2, *Coney Island, Naples, Italy, Aug. 1945.* (right) SG/PC, 5⅛ x 3⅛. **79:** SG, 5 x 3⅜, *March 31, 47, San* (2 illegible words).

80: (left) SG, 5 x 3. (right) SG/PC, 5⅛ x 3. **81:** (left) SG/PC, 5¼ x 3. (right) SG, 2⅜ x 1⅛. **82:** SG, 6 x 4½. **83:** SG, 2 5/16 x 4. **84:** (left) SG/CV, 2¼ x 3⅝. (right) TT, 3⅜ x 2¼. **85:** SG/CC, 5⅞ x 4. **87:** CB/CC, 4⅞ x 3½. **88:** (left) SG, 4¼ x 2¼. (top right) SG, 2⅜ x 4⅛. (bottom right) SG, 3 x 2. **89:** SG, 3 1/16 x 4 1/16. **90:** (top) SG, 4⅝ x 3. (bottom) SG, 2⅜ x 4. **91:** SG, 2½ x 4¼. **92:** SG, 4 x 2⅜. **93:** SG, 3 1/16 x 2 1/16. **94:** SG/PC, 5 x 3, *Baccarat, the 25 February 1911, It is to tell you that if you have a free Sunday come see us, I assure you that your visit will make us happy. I send you my picture as quartermaster-sergeant. I shall be relieved on the 1st of March and I won't be upset by it. The young man who is with me, it's the husband of one of my cousins. On this I shake your hand cordially. Your friend* (translated from the French). **95:** SG/PC, 4¾ x 3. **96:** (top left) SG, 3 x 2½, stamped: June 13, 1941. (bottom left) SG, 2⅛ x 3¼. (right) SG, 3⅛ x 2⅛. **97:** SG, 5 11/16 x 3½. **98:** (left) AL/CV, 2⅛ x 4 13/16. **98/99:** SG, 15⅝ x 21. **100:** SG/PC, 5⅛ x 3⅛, *April 17th 1927.* **101:** SG, 4 7/16 x 3¼, *B*(illegible), *the 10th Sept. 1922.* **102:** PL, 5½ x 3¾. **104:** TT, 2⅛ x 1½. **106:** SG/PC, 5⅜ x 3⅜. **108:** SG, 2⅞ x 1⅞. **111:** SG, 2 5/16 x 3¾.

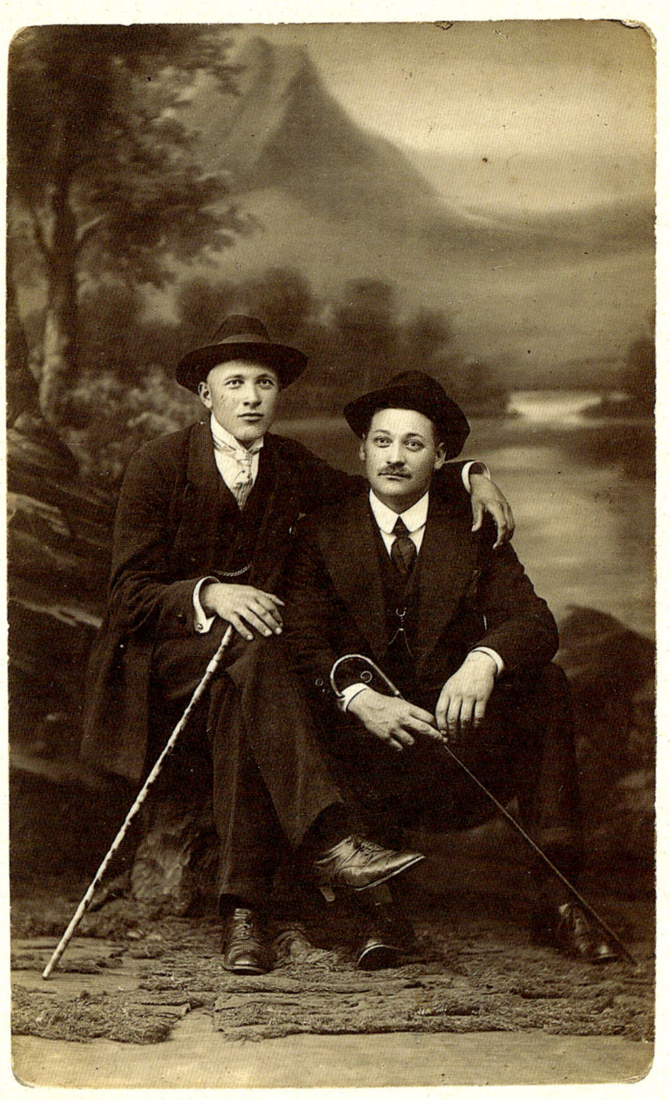

America 1911

For Further Reading

Calloway, Stephen, & David Colvin. *The Exquisite Life of Oscar Wilde.* London: Orion Books, 1997.

Chenoune, Farid. *A History of Men's Fashion.* Paris–New York: Flammarion, 1995.

Collins, Douglas. *The Story of Kodak*. New York: Harry N. Abrams, 1990.

Dalrymple, Priscilla Harris. *American Victorian Costume in Early Photographs.* New York: Dover Publications, 1991.

Donald, David Herbert. *Lincoln*. New York: Simon & Schuster, 1995.

Ellmann, Richard. *Oscar Wilde*. New York: Alfred A. Knopf, 1988.

Gardiner, James. *Who's a Pretty Boy Then? One Hundred & Fifty Years of Gay Life in Pictures.* London: Serpent's Tail, 1996.

———. *A Class Apart: The Private Pictures of Montague Glover*. London: Serpent's Tail, 1992.

Holland, Merlin. *The Wilde Album*. New York: Henry Holt, 1998.

Linkman, Audrey. *The Victorians: Photographic Portraits*. London: Tauris Parke Books, 1993.

Morgan, Hal, & Andreas Brown. *Prairie Fires and Paper Moons: The American Photographic Postcard 1900–1920*. Boston: David R. Godine Publisher, 1981.

Novotny, Ann. *Alice's World: The Life and Photography of an American Original; Alice Austen, 1866–1952*. Old Greenwich, Conn.: Chatham Press, 1976.

Oates, Stephen B. *Abraham Lincoln: The Man Behind the Myths*. New York: Harper & Row, 1984.

Reilly, James M. *Care and Identification of 19th-Century Photographic Prints.* Rochester, N.Y.: Eastman Kodak, 1986.

Rosenblum, Naomi. *A World History of Photography.* Revised edition. New York: Abbeville Press, 1984, 1989.

Rowse, A. L. *Homosexuals in History: A Study of Ambivalence in Society, Literature and the Arts.* Dorset Press/Marlboro Books, 1983.

Schmidgall, Gary. *Walt Whitman: A Gay Life.* New York: Dutton, 1997.

Spencer, Colin. *Homosexuality: A History*. London: Fourth Estate, 1995.

Whitman, Walt. *Leaves of Grass.* Philadelphia: David McKay, 1891–2.

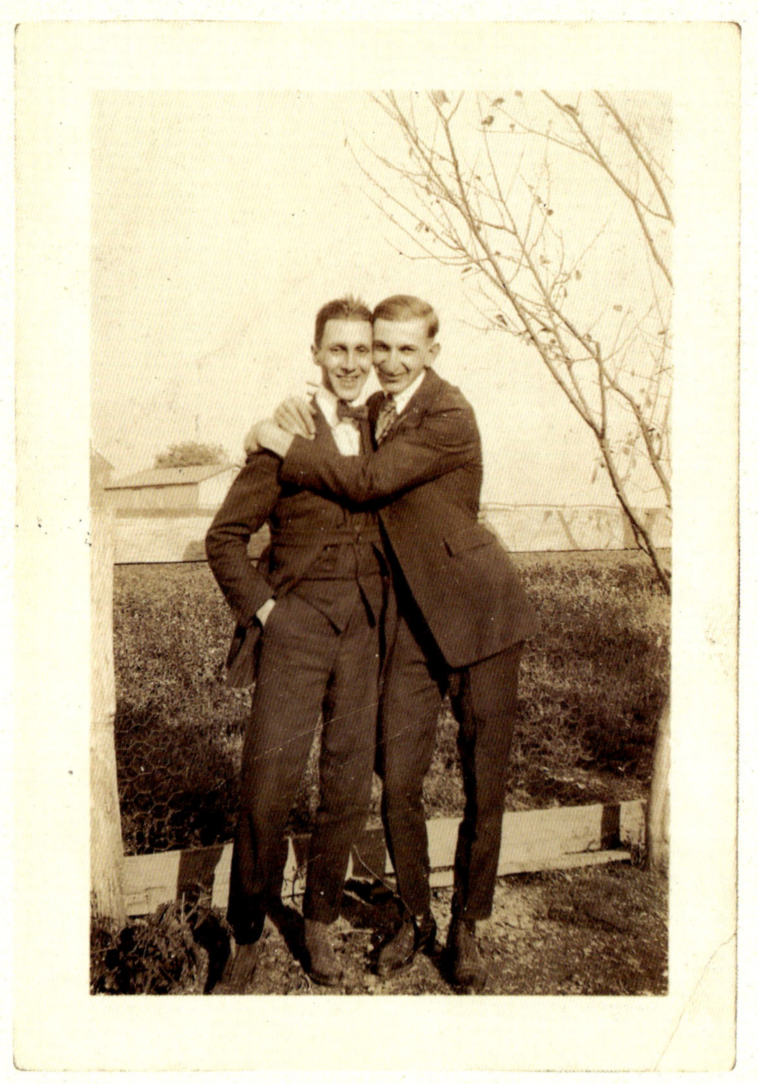

America c. 1920

Acknowledgments

Compiling a book, like collecting photographs, requires the help of others. I wish to thank the following for their generous assistance:

James Brookens, Donna Ghelerter, Jim Graham, Constantine Gorges, Michael Gray at the National Trust Fox Talbot Museum, Titi Halle, Nora Kennedy, Elizabeth Martin of the conservation department at the Victoria and Albert Museum, Steve McLure, Carl Morse, Marie Rauch, Fern Rickman, Tony Sanborn, Helene Stein, Joe Tartt, David Winter, and Angie Yun-Krent;

Richard Martin, Deirdre Donohue and Stephane Houy-Towner of the Costume Institute at the Metropolitan Museum of Art;

the staff at St. Martin's Press, especially Curt Alliaume, Robert Cloud, Karen Gillis, Sarah Rutigliano, and Michael Denneny, the visionary editor who made my dream of a book of affectionate men a reality;

Ray Roberts, who far surpassed the obligation of friendship with his constant encouragement and advice;

Ron Lieberman, a man whose love of design is second only to the love and support with which he enhances my life. He has been ably assisted with the production of *Affectionate Men* by Larry Auerbach's digital artwork, Bonnie West's prop photography, Edwin Bergman, John Gilman, Steve Guarnaccia, Robert Heide, George Hudačko, Rona Hunter, Jerry Lieberman, Eugenio Petit Jr., Richard Rogers, Tim Womack, Marc Yankus, and Vicki Gold Levi, who was the first to offer encouragement and to help visualize the formation of a book.

I wish to thank my parents for their love and constant support. They have been, and will always be, the calm in the storm known as life.

Finally, I should perhaps be most grateful to the largely unknown photographers and the men whose faces so beautifully adorn this book. I wish I could know the real stories behind the images. These photographs were once discarded and forgotten but have now been assembled into a new kind of photo album. Its contents will give pleasure to so many viewers—far more than the original photographers could have ever imagined.

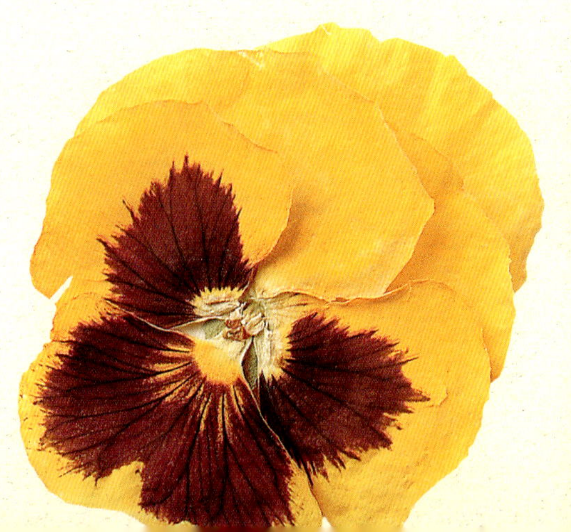

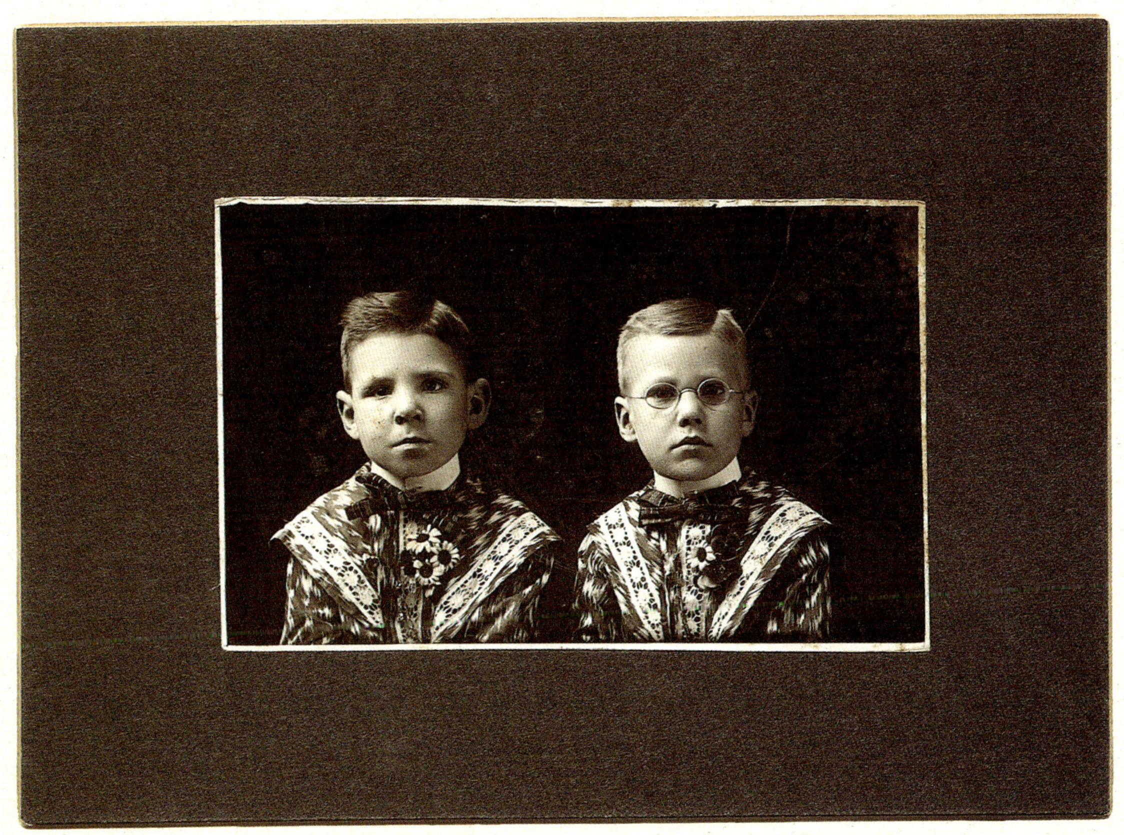

America 1910–15

AFFECTIONATE MEN:
A PHOTOGRAPHIC HISTORY OF A CENTURY OF MALE COUPLES
(1850's to 1950's).

For more information, address: St. Martin's Press, 175 Fifth Avenue, New York, N.Y. 10010.

Book and dust jacket design by Ron Lieberman.

Library of Congress Cataloging-in-Publication Data

Bush, Russell.
Affectionate Men:
a photographic history of a century of male couples, 1850's to 1950's / Russell Bush; designed by Ron Lieberman. — 1st ed.
p. cm.
ISBN 0-312-18299-6

1. Male friendship–History. 2. Male friendship–Pictorial works.
3. Gay male couples–History. 4. Gay male couples–Pictorial works.
5. Photography of men–History. I. title.

HQ1090.B87 1998 98-22815
302.3'4'081022-dc21 CIP

First Edition: October 1998

10 9 8 7 6 5 4 3 2 1

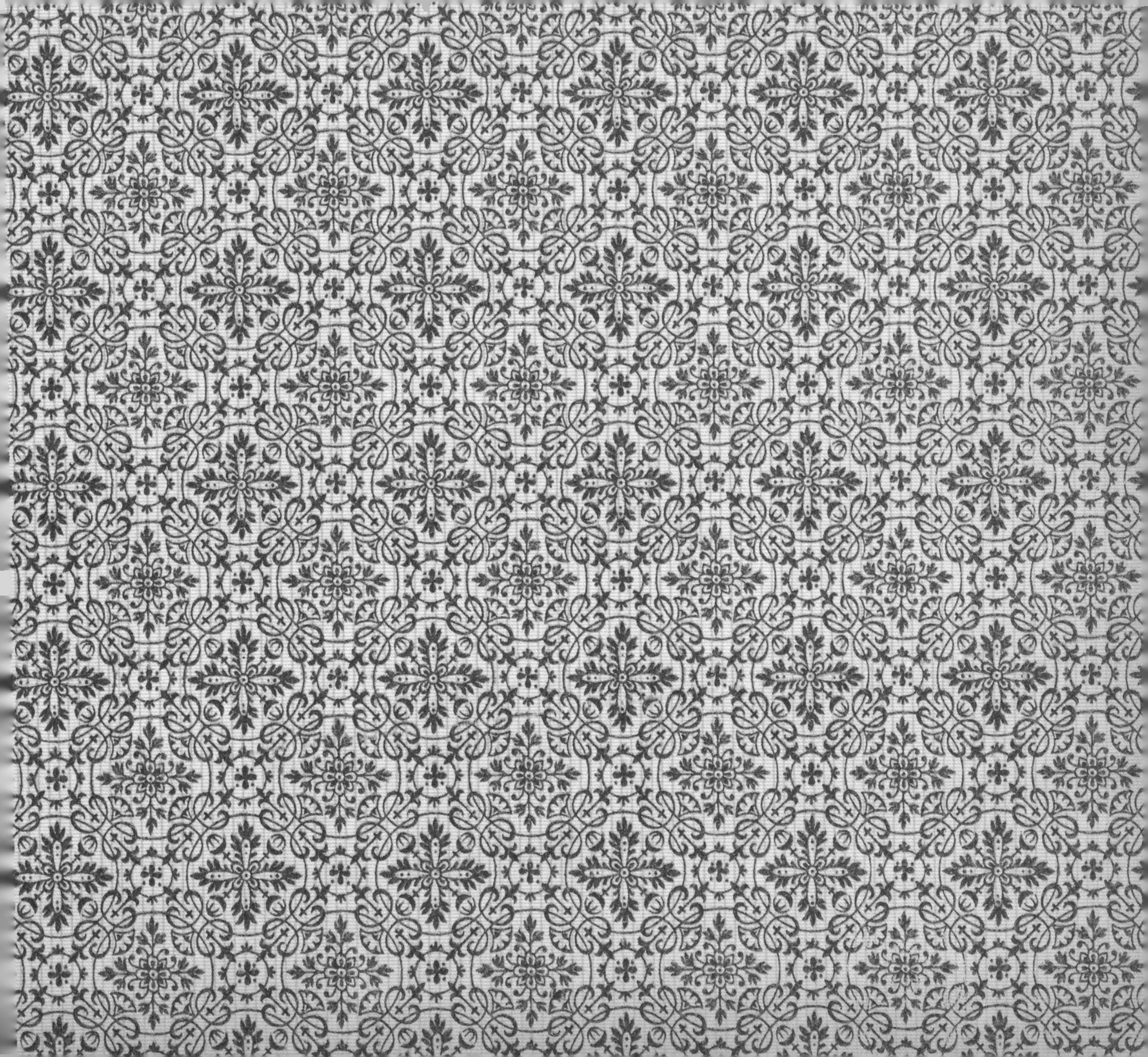

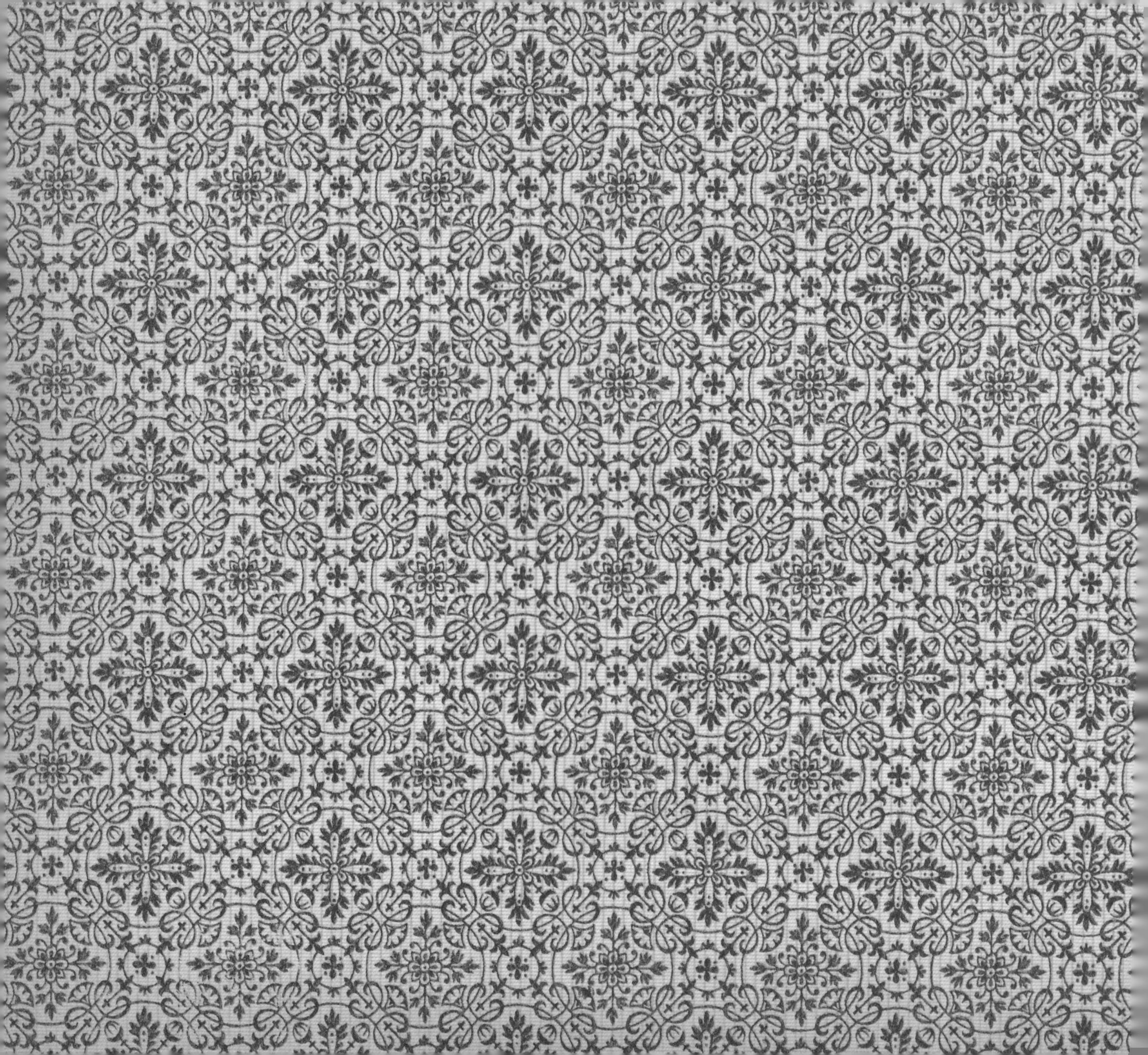